COLLECTIVE ENTREPRENEURSHIP IN A GLOBALIZING ECONOMY

COLLECTIVE ENTREPRENEURSHIP IN A GLOBALIZING ECONOMY

Panos Mourdoukoutas

Q

QUORUM BOOKS
Westport, Connecticut • London

Library of Congress Cataloging-in-Publication Data

Mourdoukoutas, Panos.
    Collective entrepreneurship in a globalizing economy / by Panos
Mourdoukoutas.
        p.   cm.
    Includes bibliographical references and index.
    ISBN 1–56720–289–6 (alk. paper)
    1. Entrepreneurship.   I. Title.
HB615.M69   1999
658.4'21—dc21   99–10408

British Library Cataloguing in Publication Data is available.

Library of Congress Catalog Card Number: 99–10408
ISBN: 1–56720–289–6

First published in 1999

Quorum Books, 88 Post Road West, Westport, CT 06881
An imprint of Greenwood Publishing Group, Inc.
www.quorumbooks.com

Printed in the United States of America

The paper used in this book complies with the
Permanent Paper Standard issued by the National
Information Standards Organization (Z39.48–1984).

10   9   8   7   6   5   4   3   2   1

To Anastasia

Contents

Exhibits

Preface

In the years of bitter struggle between capitalism and socialism, young
generations around the world were obsessed with Karl Marx and his
socialist ideas, especially those generations living in the former Soviet Republics, China, even Europe, and in what was once called the
"Third World." Posters of celebrated revolutionaries like Che Guevara,
Fidel Castro, and Mao Tse-tung decorated university walls, while
red banners and anticapitalist, antibusiness slogans colored and en-
livened union protests and popular demonstrations. Entrepreneurs
were viewed by a large part of society as ruthless exploiters, and as
the "blood suckers" of the working class and wealth accumulators
for its own sake or for conspicuous consumption.

Today, with the triumph of capitalism over socialism, with unionism in retreat, and with another Renaissance of individual freedoms
and liberties, younger generations are no longer obsessed with socialist ideals and antibusiness slogans. Their heroes and idols are no
longer celebrated revolutionaries. They are entrepreneurs like Bill
Gates, Michael Dell, and Steve Case, who have been the revolutionaries in their own industries, delivering the world new products and
businesses and creating enormous wealth for themselves, their asso-
ciates, stockholders, and society at large.

In some sense, today's admiration for entrepreneurs parallels Mark Twain's and Charles Dudley Warner's *Gilded Age*, a thirty-five-year period of growth and prosperity for the United States that had its own celebrated entrepreneurs, like Andrew Carnegie and John D. Rockefeller, at least before public opinion turned against them. Yet unlike the Gilded Age, today's obsession with individual entrepreneurs is misplaced. Behind the success of Microsoft, Dell Computer, and hundreds and thousands of other successful known and unknown corporations are not just the visible and the famous individual entrepreneurs who initiated them, but the hundreds and thousands of unknown individual entrepreneurs who collectively share the risks and the rewards from the discovery and development of new products and businesses. Windows 95, for instance, was not developed and marketed by Bill Gates alone. For practical reasons, he could not have either the time or the technical skills and expertise to write the millions of lines of software code behind the flushing screens and eye-catching images; neither would he have the marketing skills and time to persuade computer vendors and manufacturers to install a copy of the software in almost every PC that came off the manufacturing line.

Windows 95 was developed and marketed by hundreds of engineers and marketers both inside and outside Microsoft corporate boundaries, paid on the basis of performance, mostly in stock options, rather than on a flat wage basis. In this sense, each and every member of Microsoft and its partners and alliances is part of a collective entrepreneurship rather than part of a conventional hierarchical organization that divides its members into stockholders, managers, and workers, into insiders and outsiders. Each member plays a role in Microsoft entrepreneurial activities and shares the risks and the rewards from the discovery and exploitation of new business.

This does not mean that Microsoft holds referendums to decide which new products to develop or which new markets to pursue, but it has created structures that offer the opportunity to the hundreds or even thousands of hidden entrepreneurs scattered among suppliers, distributors, customers, and collaborators to come forward with the information they possess and to join forces for the discovery and exploitation of new business opportunities.

Microsoft's case is neither isolated nor unique, but part of a new trend that has shifted the focus of business organizations from management and control to entrepreneurship and creativity, which transfers technology from labs to factories and offices, delivering new products and services. This trend is particularly evident in high-technology corporations that rely heavily on the integration of technical and market information in the possession of hundreds or even thousands of professionals scattered both inside and outside the conventional corporate boundaries.

Acknowledging this new trend, a number of economists and business strategists have come up with new theories and new business strategies for the management of today's enterprises. In *Re-engineering the Corporation*, business strategists Michael Hammer and James Champy argue for a new business strategy that replaces Frederick W. Taylor's system of division of labor by individual task and its replacement by the division of labor by process. Hammer and Champy's model has in essence eliminated middle management. In *The Virtual Corporation*, Davidow and Malone argue for a new concept of enterprise, a network of corporate alliances, often among former competitors. Yet both books emphasize the managerial rather than the entrepreneurial function of the firm.

A critical appraisal and an extension of this literature, this book has a dual objective. The first objective is to address the "other side" of globalization and to point to the limitations of conventional reengineering strategies in competing in ever faster-moving and ever saturated global markets where companies compete against themselves rather than against consumers. The second objective of this book is to point to the shift of focus of business strategy from the managerial to the entrepreneurial function of the firm, and to outline a new concept of the business enterprise, collective entrepreneurship, an enterprise without internal and external boundaries, whose members share a common fate.

Acknowledgments

The author is indebted to Dimitris Alexopoulos for his assistance with some of the graphs, to Pavlos Mourdoukoutas for some of the ideas about intellectual-property-right protection in Chapter 7, and to Vicki Karlis for editorial comments.

Chapter 1 ─────────────────────────────

Collective Entrepreneurship:
The Ultimate Advantage

The history of the twentieth century has been a testing ground for innumerable theories of social and economic organization that have been tried and found wanting. The way people respond to incentives and rewards persists from generation to generation suggesting a deeply imbedded set of stabilities in human nature.

—Alan Greenspan

For almost two decades, globalization, the increasing integration and interdependence of world markets, has transformed the ways companies organize and compete with each other. Under a business strategy known as "reengineering," advanced logistics and human resource management practices have been the driving force behind operational effectiveness (lower costs and product quality improvements). In this book, we argue that, as globalization gains momentum, reengineering can no longer warrant sustainable competitive advantages, and is of little relevance to business strategy. The business strategy of the future will be one that focuses on revenue growth and on the constructive destruction of conventional corporations through collective entrepreneurship, rather than on operational effectiveness alone.

Globalization is not a new trend but the resumption of an old trend that began in the last quarter of the nineteenth century: "At the turn of the century, it seemed as if capitalism was on track to conquer the world economy, creating a global market, a market without national boundaries and government restrictions, a market where commodities and resources could flow freely both within and across national boundaries."[1] Early globalization was interrupted by excessive competition and antagonism among corporations and nations, the rise of communism and fascism, protectionism, unionism, government regulation, and the two world wars that transformed the early world economy from a single integrated global market to a fractured multinational market.

Driven by the collapse of communist and fascist regimes, the establishment of the World Trade Organization (WTO), the expansion and strengthening of regional organizations, the weakening of unions, deregulation and privatization, and the spread of information technology, today's globalization is a mixed blessing for businesses. On the bright side, globalization is a source of efficiency and opportunity, expanding sales and raising profits (Exhibit 1.1). The creation of WTO and the lifting of protectionism, for instance, let companies sell their products around the world with the same ease as in their local market, attaining economies of scale and saving billions of dollars in tariffs and bureaucratic customs procedures. The weakening of unions allowed companies a higher degree of flexibility in adjusting the quantity and quality of labor inputs to changing economic and technological conditions. The collapse of socialism expanded business horizons to former socialist countries of Eastern Europe, the former Soviet republics, and Asia, while deregulation and privatization opened up several economic sectors to private enterprises. Indeed, a number of well-known corporations from the United States, Europe, and Japan have already expanded their presence in the markets of the former socialist countries, rewarding their stockholders with higher profits, and some private corporations have entered businesses previously provided by the government or controlled by local monopolies, such as the running of prisons, community hospitals, and government recruiting services and the production

Exhibit 1.1
The Two Sides of Globalization

The Bright Side	The Dark Side
Source of New Opportunities	Excessive Capacity and Competition
Emerging Markets	New Entrants
New Products and Industries	Imitation
New Ways of Distributing Products	Market Saturation
	Product Obsolescence
Source of Efficiency	Price and Business Destruction
Lower Transaction Costs	
Lower Inventory Costs	
Reduced Response Time	
Economies of Scale	
Economies of Scope	
Expanding Sales and Profits	Rising Risks
	Increasing Difficulties in Protecting
	Intellectual Property Rights
	Lower Profit Margins

of electricity. The spread of information technology allows companies to communicate efficiently and effectively and to cut down on inventories, increase response time, find new ways to distribute their products and convey their services, and develop new products.

On the dark side, globalization is a source of compounding uncertainty manifested in excessive competition and productive capacity, rising risks, price and business destruction, and lower profit margins (see Exhibit 1.1). Specifically, globalization has let consumers "turn the tables" on producers, forcing producers to compete against each other rather than against consumers. This is especially the case for companies in industries that are at the forefront of globalization, such as automobiles, telecommunications, semiconductors, computers, and consumer electronics, where excess capacity has been driving prices sharply lower. Globalization has also intensified competition among companies and countries that produce conventional, easy to imitate products, like those produced by Southeast Asian countries and China, and this could explain the economic turmoil of the region in the later part of the 1990s. Worse, the increasing interdependence associated with globalization compounds and magnifies the risks and uncertainties for companies operating in several world markets at the same time, especially in emerging markets; that is, a downturn in one market threatens the performance of a corporation in other markets. In the later part of 1997 and in 1998, American, European, and Japanese corporations with a large presence in Southeast Asia, for instance, suffered sales and profit setbacks due to their exposure in Asian markets, and the situation only became worse in the second part of 1998, when the Asian contagion spread to Russia and to a number of Latin American countries.

Another source of uncertainty associated with globalization and the information technology that supports and reinforces it is the shortening of the life of new products, which has turned conventional durable products into perishable products. Like fresh fruits and vegetables, their value declines substantially for every extra day they stay on the shelves. This is especially the case in high-technology industries, where popular products such as computers, cellular phones, and fax machines quickly become obsolete. In such industries, obsoleteness makes it difficult for corporations to write off the cost of their investment. Worse, with the information highways carrying information momentarily around the globe, it becomes increasingly difficult for corporations to protect their most precious asset, intellectual property, especially in emerging markets of former socialist countries, where property rights have yet to be defined.

To deal with the dark side of globalization, corporations have initially undergone a managerial revolution parallel to that at the turn of the century, which gave rise to new business organizations and forms of management. Specifically, corporations have focused their competitive strategy on logistics and managerial practices that promote operational effectiveness. Under a number of popular strategies known as Total Quality Circles (TQC), Total Quality Management (TQM), and reengineering, companies have reorganized their operations by *process* rather than by *individual task* and leveled off corporate hierarchies by eliminating middle management. In addition, companies organized work teams, delegating authority to them over an array of decisions previously made by middle management. Companies further introduced state-of-the-art logistics, such as just-in-time (JIT) inventory systems, linear programming, and queuing models that cut costs and improved product quality, and incentives to reward workers and their teams on a performance rather than a flat wage basis.

In many cases, such measures have brought the desired results. In the early days of globalization, for instance, TQC and TQM gave Japanese companies a competitive advantage in a number of global industries, such as automobiles, semiconductors, machine tools, office equipment, and consumer electronics. Reengineering has been credited with the rejuvenation of American global industries and their catching up with their Japanese counterparts in the 1990s, especially in semiconductors, computer, hardware and automobiles. Reengineering is further credited with recovery in a number of European Union (EU) nations, especially Great Britain, Denmark, Spain, and Portugal, that have been quick to adjust their economies to the demands of globalization.

In spite of its success, reengineering as a business strategy is subject to a number of limitations:

- As business logistics turn more complex, it becomes increasingly more expensive and difficult for companies to adopt and adapt to their parameters, and to train their members accordingly. It is both expensive and difficult for companies, for instance, to upgrade their software from Microsoft, SAP, or Oracle while their members still strive to familiarize themselves with previous upgrades.
- As reengineering practices became universal, they can be easily transferred across companies. If every automobile company uses robots in its assembly lines and logistical techniques, such as the just-in-time inventory system, they can no longer warrant a competitor sustainable com-

petitive advantages over another. Likewise, if every company applies managerial practices, such as team work and job rotation, they cannot warrant a sustainable advantage to one competitor over another either.

- As many world markets reach saturation and competition intensifies, operational effectiveness alone is not a sufficient source of competitive advantage. If VCR and PC prices, for instance, fall faster than costs, or if consumers have reached saturation for these products, companies can no longer survive and prosper just by lowering costs or by improving product quality.

- Globalization and the spread of the information technology that supports and reinforces it turns conventional products and services obsolete altogether. Shopping on the Internet, for instance, quickly substitutes for conventional shopping; Internet investing substitutes for the conventional brokerage investing; and websites substitute for travel agencies, bookstores, flower shops, car dealerships, real estate agencies, and so on.

- Globalization and the information technology that supports and reinforces it has made the process of product development, manufacturing, and marketing a far riskier and more complicated process to be handled within the traditional internal and external corporate boundaries.

- As in many cases reengineering is associated with downsizing and layoffs, it has created friction between the winners, stockholders, and the losers, middle management and labor.

- By replacing middle management with working teams, reengineering has lowered the boundaries between labor and management, and between management and stockholders, but it didn't advance far enough. Reengineering still retained the boundaries between management and stockholders and between labor and stockholders, and the boundaries between suppliers, manufacturers, distributors, and retailers.

In short, as globalization begins to show more of its dark side, it is changing the number of players, the rules, and the strategies of the market game at an unprecedented pace, creating a Schumpeterian regime of perpetual constructive destruction of industries and individual businesses. To compete efficiently and effectively under the new regime, companies must reach beyond operational effectiveness and reengineering; they must refocus their strategy from operational effectiveness, from low cost–high quality products to revenue growth. But how can companies expand revenues in saturated world markets crowded with even more competitors, falling prices, and with products turning obsolete faster than ever?

Certainly, raising revenues is a far more difficult task than cutting costs or improving product quality, especially in a Schumpeterian regime. Nevertheless, companies can raise revenues by transferring and replicating that world inside their own organization; that is, by constructively destroying their own business and abandoning conventional business and products that have either become the target of imitation or turned obsolete altogether and replacing them with new ones with little or no competition.[2] To put it differently, corporations can raise revenues through strategic innovations (i.e., by turning market niches into mass markets and by forming strategic alliances for the exploitation of new business opportunities).

Pursuing a competitive strategy of constructive destruction is easier said than done, for a number of reasons. First, the abandonment of traditional product and business lines creates redundant resources that cannot be deployed to new business lines overnight. This is especially the case for workers and managers who lack the skills to perform the new tasks required in the new product and business lines. Worse, those workers may have to wait quite some time before the new businesses are developed and even may be replaced by newly recruited workers who possess such skills. In this sense, constructive destruction of business creates winners and losers and internal friction far more extensive and pervasive than reengineering and threatens to derail the entire process of organizational development and growth.

Second, the discovery and exploitation of new businesses requires a less structured working environment where employees are free to experiment with new ideas that may upset the status quo, an environment that replaces order with disorder that, if unchecked, could threaten the stability and cohesion of the entire organization. This is especially the case in large established corporations where management is a separate entity and often detached from stockholders. Why should management take chances, replacing established businesses with new ones?

Third, the discovery and the exploitation of new businesses and products requires the integration of market and technical information that is usually scattered inside and outside the conventional corporate boundaries, among stockholders, managers, workers, suppliers, distributors, and customers. The development of software products, for instance, takes the integration of market and technical information scattered across hundreds of engineers and marketers both inside and outside the conventional boundaries of software corporations. Similarly, the design and development of a new PC requires the integration of market and technical information that cannot be owned or controlled by one individual alone, or amassed in an "ivory research tower" of a single corporation. In most cases, market information is scattered across marketing departments, distribution centers, warehouses, retail outlets, and, of course, customers. Technical information is scattered both inside and outside the corporation, in its own production and research centers, in government laboratories, and even in the laboratories of the company's competitors.

In view of these difficulties in pursuing a strategy of constructive destruction, competing in global markets is reduced to an art, the art of constructive destruction management:

- The minimization of friction between winners and losers; the planning of change; the spread of risks and rewards; the raising of support for change.
- The balancing of concentric forces that pull the organization toward order and conformity and centrifugal forces that pull the organization toward chaos and creativity.
- The integration of market and technical information for the discovery and exploitation of new business.

But how can corporations pursue the constructive destruction of their business? How can they minimize the friction between winners and losers? How can corporations balance chaos and creativity against order and conformity? How can they integrate market and technical information? By undergoing another revolution, an entrepreneurial revolution that reunites entrepreneurship and management with ownership as it existed in individual capitalism of the preindustrial and early industrial era; a revolution that transforms conventional enterprises into entrepreneurial networks, which we call *collective entrepreneurships*. But can one turn the clock back? Can large corporations be run as individual entrepreneurships?

Certainly not. Though an entrepreneurial revolution sounds realistic for small-scale start-up enterprises, such as proprietorships and partnerships where owner–entrepreneurs are directly engaged in management and have frequent and direct contacts with their workers, suppliers, and customers, it does not sound as realistic for large corporations where entrepreneurship is separated from management and labor. In addition, collective entrepreneurship in large enterprises sounds similar to the concept of the collective enterprises of the failed socialist systems and that makes business strategists uneasy. How can large hierarchical corporations turn into collective entrepreneurships? How do collective entrepreneurships differ from collective enterprises of the former socialist countries?

Large corporations can turn themselves into collective entrepreneurships by lowering the internal boundaries that for decades have separated stockholders from managers, and managers from workers, uniting entrepreneurship with the other human resources, management, and labor. Lowering the internal boundaries of conventional corporations and turning them into collective entrepreneurships may not always be sufficient for the discovery and exploitation of new business, however. This is especially the case for the development of complex products or for assuming the increased risks associated with entry into emerging markets. In these cases, collective entrepreneurship may have to be extended beyond the external boundaries of conventional corporations in two directions: vertically, between producers and their suppliers, distributors, and retailers; and horizontally, between suppliers, producers, distributors, and retailers.

The lowering of internal and external boundaries of conventional corporations challenges a number of familiar concepts of corporate capitalism; "stockholders," "managers," "workers," "firm," and the concept of the "industry." With the lowering of internal corporate boundaries, for instance, stockholders cannot be defined just as passive capital owners who delegate authority to professional managers, who in turn assign work to workers. Stockholders should be defined as active capital owners who manage the corporation and perform the work to be done, as it existed in individual capitalism that preceded corporate capitalism. In this way, stockholders no longer just own, managers no longer just manage, and workers no longer just get the job done. Workers, managers, and stockholders can communicate directly with each other, sharing important market and technical information. They participate in the decision-making process and share the risks and the rewards associated with such partnership.

With the lowering of external boundaries, firms can no longer be defined as separate hierarchical structures, but as networks of entrepreneurs, each performing one or more roles in the product supply chain. Industries can no longer be defined as a collection of distinct and separate entities competing with each other. Network members may both compete and cooperate with each other for the development of new products and businesses. Producers, for instance, can monitor inventories on behalf of their clients, tuning their own production schedules accordingly. Distributors can perform the assembly for their clients. Retailers can provide producers with useful marketing information for product cost and quality improvements. Two competing producers can cooperate with each other for the development of new products or for cracking an emerging market. In this sense, firms do not just produce, distribute, or retail; they do not just compete with each other. They also cooperate with each other; they are collective entrepreneurships in the development and the exploitation of new businesses that take resources which cannot be found within conventional boundaries or assume risks that cannot be borne by a single corporation; they share information, resources, and wealth. In this sense, collective entrepreneurship is more of an informal community of common fate and less of a formal and well-structured enterprise, an issue to be further elaborated later.

Though similar to collective enterprises of the former socialist economies, collective entrepreneurship differs from collective enterprises in a number of respects. First, collective entrepreneurships are fluid and less structured organizations owned and controlled by their members, separately rather than collectively, and they are at the whim of market forces rather than rigid hierarchical corporations under the tight grip of central planners and government bureaucrats. Second, as fluid and less structured organizations, collective entrepreneurships cultivate and nourish individual creativity and imagination rather than bureaucratic conformity and complacency of its members. Third, by contrast to the members of socialist enterprises who share the rewards but not the risks of collective ownership, the members of a collective entrepreneurship share both the risks and the rewards associated with the discovery and exploitation of business opportunities and are accountable for any failures.

In short, the intensification of competition brought about by globalization creates institutional mutations and permutations that blur the distinction between conventional hierarchical corporations, proprietorships, and partnerships, and the distinction between markets and hierarchies. Institutional mutations and permutations, in turn, dictate a reevaluation and redefinition of the concept of conventional corporation altogether. Instead of viewing corporations as orderly managerial units that allocate resources in the production of given products, corporations should be viewed as disorderly entrepreneurial units on a steady lookout for genuine business opportunities for the replacement and replenishment of their business. Even more, as human capital embedded in professionals is the ultimate source of sustainable competitive advantage, collective entrepreneurship should be seen as a network, a community of entrepreneurs sharing a common destiny, a common fate. In this sense, entrepreneurial networks can be seen as fluid organizational structures consisting of a core unit and peripheral units, enjoying both economies of scale and economies of scope. The core unit handles issues that are conducive to economies of scale, such as marketing, advertising, and financing, develops the network vision (mission and core values), and allocates the roles among network members. In performing its role, each network unit can compete or cooperate with other networks (see Exhibit 1.2). In practice, the core unit could be a large corporation, like IBM, Motorola, Sony, or Nokia, that handles the invention or innovation of new products and stands behind the final product, while the peripheral units could consist of alliances of the core corporation that handle mass manufacturing, assembly, distribution, and retailing. These alliances can, in turn, expand or contract and the allocation of roles among members can change in response to market conditions. In some cases, the core of the network could be a dis-

Exhibit 1.2
Entrepreneurial Networks: Cooperation and Competition

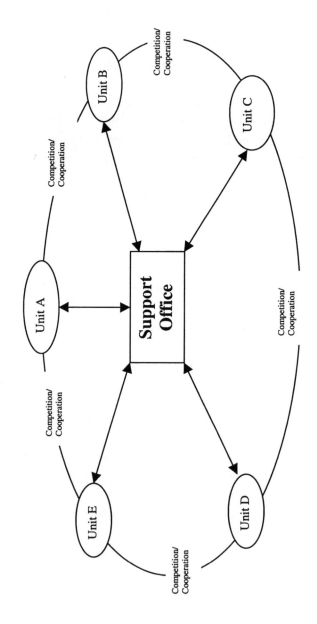

tributor or a trade company that coordinates consumption and production and even assembles products. In other cases, the core of the
network could be a retailer or a supplier. This means that, in contrast
to conventional corporations, a single model alone cannot describe
the business strategy of entrepreneurial networks.

Depending on the nature of the relations between the core and its
peripheral units, relations among peripheral units can be contractual
and noncontractual. Contractual entrepreneurial networks are short-
term, formal, and explicit agreements regarding the purpose of their
formation, their duration, and the contribution of resources of each
member and the allocation of the expected rewards. In the filmmaking industry, for instance, contractual networks are formed by writers, producers, actors, and so on for specific projects and dissolved
after the project has been completed. In the book publishing industry, entrepreneurial networks are formed among authors, editors,
publishers, distributors, and retailers. Contractual networks may be
limited to private parties or may extend to government entities. In
the United States, for instance, entrepreneurial networks are primarily
limited to private companies, with the exception of nonprofit research
institutions, such as universities and government agencies that collaborate with private companies. In Europe, entrepreneurial networks
are often mixed. They include private corporations and government
agencies, especially semiprivatized government monopolies.

Noncontractual entrepreneurial networks are networks based on
long-term informal, implicit, and vague agreements regarding the
purpose of their formation, the duration, and the contribution and the
rewards of each member. As was the case with contractual entrepreneurial networks, noncontractual entrepreneurial networks can be
formed among private parties or among private parties and government agencies. In Japan, for instance, entrepreneurial networks are
formed among large enterprise groups known as Keiretsu groups,
often cooperating with nonprofit organizations and with the Minis-
try of Trade and Industry (MITI), which acts as a coordinator of R&D
among the groups. In Southeast Asia, entrepreneurial networks are
formed among extended family members with close contacts to government agencies, especially state-controlled financial institutions.[3]

In a few words, as globalization begins to show more of its other side of excess capacity, price, and business destruction, companies can no longer gain sustainable competitive advantages through strategies that pursue operational effectiveness alone. Instead, companies must enhance and expand their revenues through the management of the constructive destruction of their business (i.e., the abandonment of their mature business and its replacement with new emerging business). Such a strategy can be implemented through organizational mutations and permutations, which turn corporations from hierarchical managerial units to entrepreneurial networks, communities of common fate, sharing the risks and rewards associated with the discovery and exploitation of new businesses. In some cases, entrepreneurial networks can be extended outside the conventional boundaries of the corporation, vertically to suppliers, distributors, and customers, and horizontally to former competitors. In such networks, the focus of business strategy of collective entrepreneurships should not be on the division of labor by task or process but on the division of entrepreneurship among their members. In either case, the strategy of collective entrepreneurship is subjected to its own limitations, namely the shortage of human talent, the difficulty of protecting intellectual property, especially in emerging market economies, and the conflicting roles among the members of entrepreneurial networks.

Arguing this contention, this book is in two parts. The first part addresses in more detail the characteristics of the "other side" of globalization and the limitations of business reengineering and operational effectiveness as a source of sustainable competitive advantages. The second part extends the discussion beyond reengineering and operational effectiveness to the constructive destruction of businesses and the strategy of collective entrepreneurship.

Chapter 2 discusses in more detail the other side of globalization, the intensification of competition, and falling prices and profit margins, and explores implications for business strategy. Chapter 3 is a discussion of the limits of reengineering and the bounds of the competitive strategy of operational effectiveness. Chapter 4 looks beyond reengineering to strategies that focus on revenue growth through the constructive destruction of businesses, especially strategic innovations and the integration of market and technical information. Chapter 5 outlines the concept of collective entrepreneurship and compares and contrasts it with individual entrepreneurship. Chapter 6 relates the concept of collective entrepreneurship to the concept of the community of common fate, corporate vision, and the division of roles. Chapter 7 discusses the limitations of constructive destruction management and collective entrepreneurship, and Chapter 8 ends the discussion with a summary and some conclusions.

NOTES

1. Arayama and Mourdoukoutas, 1999a.
2. In technical terms, this means the shift from elastic to inelastic products.
3. Arayama and Mourdoukoutas, 1999b.

PART I

The Other Side of Globalization and the Limits of Reengineering

As today's globalization begins to show more of its dark side to business, as competition intensifies and risks rise, the business strategy of operational effectiveness and the managerial revolution that fueled it have already had their place in history. Many of the principles behind the operational effectiveness strategies of TQC, TQM, and reengineering have been broadly diffused throughout the global economy. They have become standard practices, and, although still necessary, they can no longer be a sufficient source of sustainable competitive advantages.

Chapter 2 —————————————————————

The Other Side of Globalization: Price and Business Destruction

The net creates a market too perfect for profits.
—Robert Kuttner

Man must be more than a collator, a venerator of what has been.
He must create history for ages yet to be. If he may look upon
the past, he must, like Janus, have a face on both sides of his
head that he may be always apprehending the future as well.
—James Roscoe Day

Some believe that history repeats itself, that today's globalization is
the resumption of an old trend that began in the last quarter of the
nineteenth century but was interrupted by the rise of protectionism,
unionism, government regulation, and especially the two world wars
that devastated the world community. Others believe that history does
not repeat itself and that today's globalization is an entirely new trend,
that today's global corporations are the de facto guarantors of world
peace and prosperity, and, therefore, globalization can continue its
advance forever.

Irrespective of which view one shares, today's globalization is not
as rosy and cozy a system as it is often portrayed in popular publications. It is not just about new frontiers and friction-free markets, en-

hanced business opportunities and soaring financial markets. It is also an obscure system of price and business destruction brought about by the opening of national and local markets to competition, and by the spread of information technology that has eliminated the information vacuum that often gives an advantage to one firm over another. Globalization is a system of perpetual self-destruction of conventional products, ways of doing business, and competitive strategies and practices—a system of friction between winners and losers. The opening of national and local markets, for instance, has destroyed local monopolies in telecommunications and utilities, driving prices and profit margins lower. The spread of information technology has eliminated scores of industries and jobs in factories and offices, and the Internet is quickly eliminating scores of businesses and jobs in finance, marketing, and retailing.

In this sense, today's globalization is indeed similar to that of the last century, when the creation of an open world-market economy and the improvements and extension of the transportation system eliminated local monopolies, stimulated competition, and changed the structure of global industries. Today's globalization is also similar to early globalization in two other respects: the uneven distribution of growth and income across individuals and regions, and the intensification of competition and the price and business destruction associated with it.

An inquiry into the "other side" of globalization, this chapter discusses how the intensification of competition and the business destruction associated with it are changing the rules of the economic game. In particular, the chapter compares and contrasts the price and business destruction of today's globalization with that of early globalization, and explores its implications for business strategy.

INTENSIFICATION OF COMPETITION AND RISING RISKS

Ever since the publication of *The Wealth of Nations*, economists have been envisioning a capitalist system consisting of friction-free markets; that is, markets made up of a large number of well-informed suppliers and buyers free to trade with each other. Such a system, economists argue, compels sellers to be responsive to consumer demands and to be efficient (i.e., allocate resources to goods and services that consumers value the most and deliver these goods and services at the best quality and the lowest cost). In this sense, friction-free markets promote the cause for a wealthy and prosperous society, measured by the quantity and the quality of commodities its consumers can enjoy within a world of scarcity of economic resources. As John Bates Clark put it almost a century ago

[Competition] causes a race of improvement in which eager rivals strive with each other to see who can get the best result from a day's labor. It puts the producer where he must be enterprising or drop out of the race. He must invent machines and processes or adopt them as others discover them. He must organize, explore markets, and study consumer wants. He must keep abreast of a rapidly moving procession if he expects to continue long to be a producer at all.[1]

This was particularly the case in the last quarter of the nineteenth century, the days of early globalization. As Thorstein Veblen puts it, "That period which has been called the 'era of free competition' was marked by a reasonably free competitive production of goods for the market, the profits of the business to be derived from competitive underselling. . . . It meant a competition between producing-sellers and so far as the plan was operative it inured to the benefit of the consumers."[2]

Carl Snyder is more assertive and more supportive of "free competition," especially the accumulation of capital, the division of labor, and the efficient utilization of a society's resources:

This system or mode of industrial and social organization, has achieved in recent centuries results that must remain spectacular in the last degree, since nothing like it has ever before been known in history. This accumulation and utilization of capital, the "division of labor" it provides, and the utilization of every kind of talent and unusual capacity, has led to a volume and variety of production of goods, conveniences and satisfactions that almost defy enumeration.[3]

Friction-free markets and social prosperity come at a cost, however: the uneven development of industries and the uncertainty created by the bouncing of markets between surpluses and shortages created by the massive migration of competitors from nonprofitable to profitable industries. As Maurice Dobb put it

Throughout its history (certainly since the industrial revolution and perhaps to some extent before) capitalism has shown striking unevenness of development, not only in the sense that different sectors and regions have grown at different rates, but in the sense that the system as a whole has shown a marked rhythm of fluctuation between alternating periods of expansion and retardation and contraction.[4]

Alan Greenspan is more specific about the causes of business fluctuations, especially the causes of crises: "[Capitalist] crises arise on occasion when confidence fails and is replaced by fear and loss of trust, including a vicious cycle of retrenchment in economic activity and government endeavors to counter it."[5]

Entry of new competitors in saturated markets, for instance, creates excess capacity, driving prices and profits lower and forcing inefficient companies out of these markets. The exit of firms from nonprofitable industries pushes markets to an opposite state: shortages and rising prices. Yet for most of their history, especially from the second decade of the twentieth century to the early 1970s, real world markets did not function as envisioned by mainstream economists; they were not friction free.[6] With a few exceptions, buyers and sellers were neither well informed nor free to trade with each other. National barriers, such as tariffs, quotas, and customs regulations, constrained the freedom of crossborder transactions between buyers and sellers. Local barriers, such as insufficient transportation and communication infrastructure and government regulations, constrained the flow of products from one location to another. Size, distance, and insufficient information gave one seller an advantage over another, creating even more market barriers that protected companies from potential competitors. In such a world, corporations applied their power to restrict output and raise prices. As Thorstein Veblen observed

Doubtless, such freely competitive production and selling prevailed only within reasonable bounds even in the time when may have been the rule in industrial business, and with the passage of time and the approaching saturation of the market the reasonable bounds gradually grew narrower and stricter. The manner of conducting the business passed by insensible degrees into a new order, and it became an increasingly patent matter-of-course for business enterprise in this field consistently to pursue the net gain by maintaining prices and curtailing output.

In this sense, business enterprises pursued profit rather than consumer welfare, turning producers against consumers rather than against each other. "It is not that competition ceased when this 'competitive system' fell into decay, but only that the incidence of it shifted. The competition which then used to run mutually between the producing-sellers has since then increasingly come to run between the business community on the one side and the consumers on the other."[7]

In other words, friction-free capitalism that early on created an integrated global market and forced producers to compete with each other for the benefit of consumers and the society at large eventually created a fractured multinational market and turned into friction capitalism that has provided for sanctuaries that shelter corporations from potential competitors and the price destruction associated with it. Trade barriers, for instance, have sheltered inefficient industries of one country from the efficient industries of another country. Government regulations sheltered a number of inefficient local monopolies from the efficient companies of another location. In the U.S. telecommunications industry, for instance, government regulation sheltered AT&T from competition long-distance services for years, and the Baby Bells from competition in local services. In this way, the "emphasis gradually shifted away from simple growth in output to the control of whole industries, the rationalization of competition, and the imposition of order in the formerly individualistic producers."[8]

The increasing integration of national and local markets brought about by the resumption of globalization since the late 1970s and the spread of information technology that supports and reinforces it has lead to an invasion of market sanctuaries, however. From telecommunications to airlines and even utilities, customers can shop around for the best service at the lowest cost. In the U.S. telecommunications industry, for instance, AT&T has already lost its long-distance monopoly to newcomers MCI and Sprint, and in local service the Baby Bells are about to yield to new competitors. In Europe, especially in Great Britain, Germany, and France, British Telecom,

Deutsche Telekom, and French Telecom have lost their sanctuaries, and are now competing head to head with each other.

As globalization and the spread of information technology gained momentum in the 1990s, their impact extended beyond the elimination of market monopolies to the constructive destruction of businesses. As Richard D'Aveni observes, "Market stability is threatened by short product life cycles, short product design cycles, new technologies, frequent entry by unexpected outsiders, repositioning by incumbents, and radical redefinition of market boundaries as diverse industries merge."[9] In some industries, such as investing and retailing, globalization and information technology allow buyers and suppliers to communicate directly and momentarily with each other, eliminating the information vacuum that often gave advantage to one supplier over another. A computer and a modem are all buyers need to visit virtual markets around the globe and execute transactions just with a simple keyboard stroke. On their part, sellers are in a position to monitor their production and inventories and follow their buyers' preferences momentarily, reaching out to new consumers beyond their own local market.

In short, globalization and information technology may not have turned markets completely friction free, as Adam Smith and his disciples envisioned them, but they have brought them very close to that realm. This means that consumers can enjoy a larger quantity of better-quality products, especially in mature economies where consumers have reached saturation. What is good news for consumers is not necessary good news for corporations, however, which face the prospect of price and business destruction and falling profits.

PRICE AND BUSINESS DESTRUCTION
AND FALLING PROFITS

The intensification of competition brought about by globalization and new technology has created an entirely new regime for businesses, especially those mostly exposed to global competition. In industry after industry, and in country after country, prices are falling and are falling faster than ever. In fact, according to a 1998 Prudential Securities survey, 40 percent of industries covered by the firm's analysts experienced price declines, while 26.4 percent experienced price increases.[10] In just seven months, from November 1997 to May 1998, the index of twenty-two commodities followed by Goldman Sachs & Co. fell by 25 percent.[11] Price destruction has been evident for much longer in a number of industries that are exposed to global competition, such as computer disks, PCs, software, frozen dinners, diapers, and even medical equipment, food, and tobacco.[12] Price destruction is also evident in the semiconductor industry, where prices have been falling sharply and consistently, year after year, since the mid-1980s (see Exhibit 2.1). Worse, in some industries, like U.S. telecommunications, price destruction is expected to accelerate, driving prices down by 20 percent annually, and by the year 2000 to 1 percent of what they were in 1987.[13]

Price destruction is not confined to one region or one country; it extends to almost every region and every country that is part of the global economy. In Europe, for instance, prices are falling across the board. In the travel industry, thanks to startups, Rome–Milan airfares have dropped from $130 to $82, Paris–Toulouse from $88 to $70, and London–Barcelona from $358 to $165.[14] In the telecommunications industry, telephone rates have declined by 10 percent annually in recent years. In Germany alone, telephone rates have dropped by 39 percent since the local markets opened to competition in 1998. In Great Britain, telephone rates have fallen by 35 percent, and electric and gas rates have also fallen by 35 percent.[15]

Price destruction is most evident in countries and regions that seemed to be the earlier winners of globalization, such as Japan and Southeast Asia, especially in countries that compete on the basis of imitation rather than innovation, such as South Korea, Malaysia, Thailand, Indonesia, and China. In Japan, asset depression, deregulation, and competition from Southeast Asian countries have caused *kakaku*, price destruction, which has touched almost every sector of the economy. In fact, Japan is the only industrial country that has experienced deflation since 1930s.[16] In China, competition from other Southeast Asian countries and market saturation for labor-intensive products has been driving its export prices lower. Between 1985 and 1995, for

Exhibit 2.1
Summary Price Index for Microprocessors

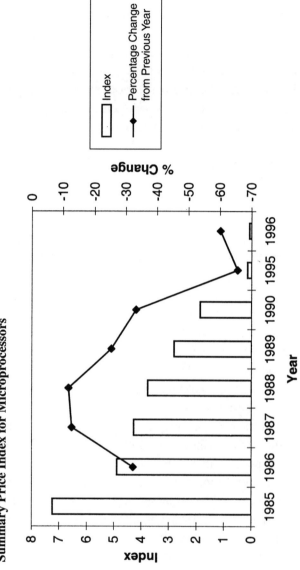

Source: Data taken from Bruce T. Grimm, "Price Indexes for Selected Semiconductors, 1974–1996," *Survey of Current Business*, February 1998, p. 23.

instance, a period that China experienced a nearly 40-percent devaluation of her currency, the export unit value of wristwatches dropped by 66 percent, the export unit values of clocks dropped by 47 percent, the export unit value of electric fans dropped by 44 percent, and the export unit value of dry cells dropped by 32 percent. In fact, over this period only one Chinese commodity, cameras, escaped price destruction and even registered substantial price appreciation (see Exhibit 2.2).[17] In Taiwan, a slowdown in computer sales and the Korean crisis have created a glut in the semiconductor market that has pushed prices sharply lower at a time the country was trying to become a major semiconductor player.[18]

Price destruction is not new. In fact, as suggested earlier, the world economy has been bouncing back and forth between price destruction and price outbursts. Price destruction has often been associated with periods of increasing market integration, such as that of the early globalization of the last quarter of the nineteenth century that brought an end to the Gilded Age. As Margaret Levenstein observes, "As late nineteenth-century manufacturers attempted to take advantage of the opportunities presented by the decline in transportation costs and the opening up of new markets, they were confronted with a new problem—real price competition, and often dramatic decline in price."[19] Specifically, the composite Consumer Price Index fell from $1.96 in 1866 to $1.21 by 1915 (see Exhibit 2.3). Characteristically, the price of bromine fell from $4.50 in 1865 to 20 cents by 1884; the price for salt fell from 67 cents per barrel in 1882 to 23 cents by 1905;[20] and the price of gasoline from 25.7 cents in 1871 to 4.9 cents in 1895.[21] Price outbursts are associated with periods of increasing disintegration of markets by the rise of tariffs and government regulation such as the period from 1909 to 1929 (see Exhibit 2.3).

The intensification of competition is not confined to products; it extends to services, too. In brokerage, for instance, online trading replaces both traditional and discount brokerages, and threatens to replace the concept of the traditional stock exchange as we know it. Online trading increased from about 2,000 subscribers in 1996 to 6 million by 1998, and is expected to reach 14 million by 2002.[22] In retailing, virtual shopping centers are replacing actual shopping cen-

Exhibit 2.2
China's Export Unit Values

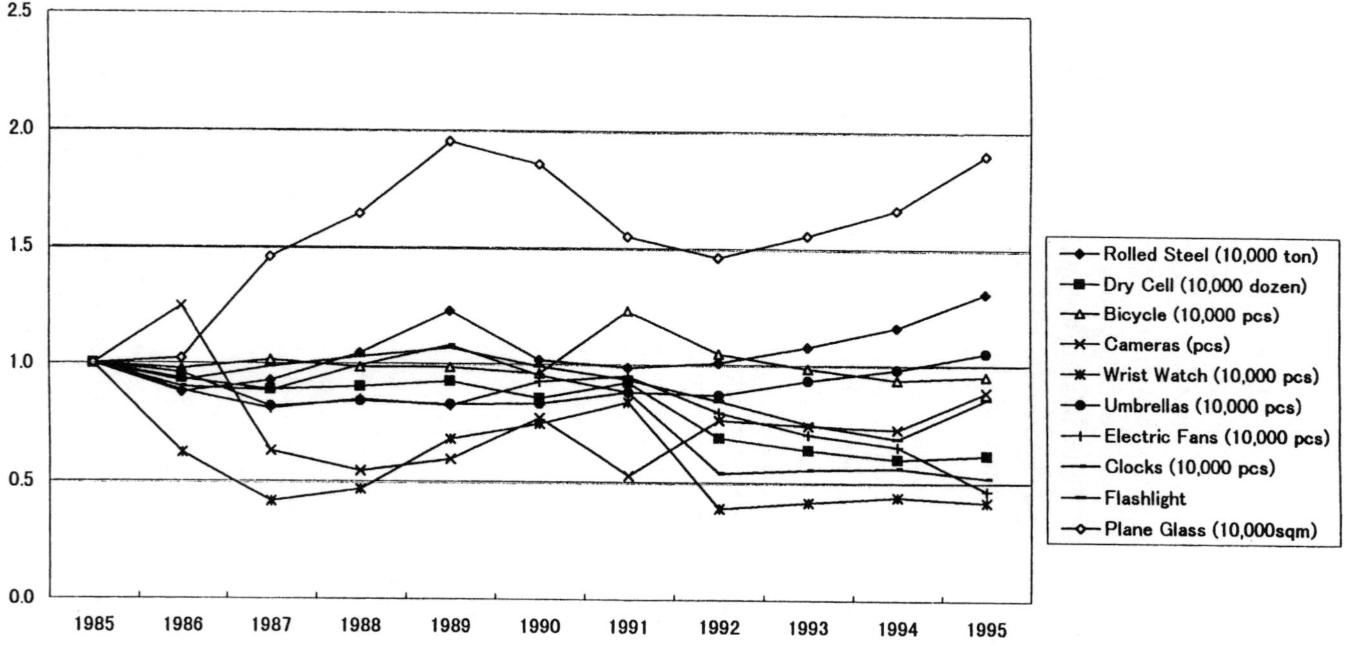
2.5
2.0
1.5
1.0
0.5
0.0
1985
1986
1987
1988
1989
1990
1991
1992
1993
1994
1995
Rolled Steel (10,000 ton)
Dry Cell (10,000 dozen)
Bicycle (10,000 pcs)
Cameras (pcs)
Wrist Watch (10,000 pcs)
Umbrellas (10,000 pcs)
Electric Fans (10,000 pcs)
Clocks (10,000 pcs)
Flashlight
Plane Glass (10,000sqm)

Exhibit 2.3
The Value of a Dollar, 1860–1989

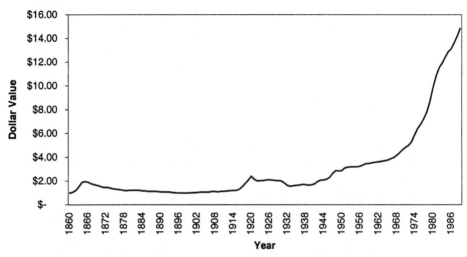

Source: Data taken from Scott Derks, ed., *The Value of a Dollar, 1860–1989* (Detroit: Gale Research, 1994).

ters. In books and music, Internet sales approached $200 million in 1997 and are expected to exceed $1 billion by 2001. In gifts and flowers, Internet sales exceeded $100 million in 1997 and are expected to exceed $500 million by 2001. In consumer electronics, Internet sales approached $15 million in 1997 and are expected to reach $150 million by 2001.[23]

As was the case with price destruction, business destruction is not driven just by the Internet. It is also driven by deregulation and the blending of technologies that used to separate one from another, such as the blending of cable and telecommunications technologies that let cable providers and telecommunications providers invade each other's markets and the blending of computer hardware and entertainment hardware that let computer makers and entertainment hardware makers invade each other's markets.

In short, the intensification of competition brought about by globalization has created a near-friction-free global economy, leading to excess capacity and price wars that have hurt sales and corporate profits. Once a Wall Street high-flier, Rubbermaid is a case in point. For years the company enjoyed its position in a fragmented multinational market, charging a premium for its brand-name products. Globalization and the intensification of competition associated with it has changed all that, however. The company's sales have flattened, its profits slumped, and its stock price fallen down to earth. As Timothy Aeppel observed, "Part of Rubbermaid's problem relates to changes beyond its control in the retail industry. There was a time when its powerful brand name let it charge a big premium. But with pressure from retailers to discount and a growing number of challengers anxious to steal Rubbermaid's business, the company has had to cut prices or risk losing shelf space."[24]

Rubbermaid's case is not unique. Corporate profits have fallen sharply in the diskdrive industry where well-known companies such as Western Digital, Seagate Technologies, Quantum Corporation, and Iomega registered big losses in late 1997 and early 1998. Over the same period, corporate profits have also suffered in the computer chip industry, where microprocessor maker Intel barely broke even, while memory chip maker Micron Technology registered huge losses. Corporate profits also took a plunge in a number of companies with large exposure to Asian markets, such as Boeing, Procter & Gamble, Caterpillar, 3M, and Nike. But even in the service industry, such as entertainment, the intensification of competition has been squeezing profit margins.[25] And industry observers are growing pessimistic about profit margins in the auto industry, which has been adding capacity at a fast pace.[26] A confirmation of such pessimism about profit prospects of global corporations was the August 1998 mini–stock market crash that shaved off close to 20 percent of U.S. stock prices.

Not all companies have been touched by the intensification of competition. In fact, a number of high-technology companies have managed to escape price destruction and even raise prices. Network equipment makers, such as Lucent Technologies and Cisco Systems, have been enjoying hefty profit margins. Software makers such as Microsoft and SAP, Internet providers such as America Online, and direct computer sellers such as Dell Computer, have also fared well. To this list, one can add home building supplier Home Depot and the Starbucks coffee shop chain. How did these companies escape price destruction? What business strategies did they follow?

IMPLICATIONS FOR BUSINESS STRATEGY

To say that the resumption of globalization and the spread of the information technology that supports and reinforces it have revolutionized the ways companies organize and compete with each other is an understatement. As discussed briefly in Chapter 1, in the 1970s and 1980s, the first period of today's globalization, under a set of strategies known as TQC, TQM, and reengineering companies have undergone a managerial revolution that shifted the focus of business enterprise away from organizing their businesses by the principles of the division of labor by task to the division of labor by process. Specifically, corporations have taken a number of measures to improve operational effectiveness; that is, to raise productivity and cut costs and improve product quality (see Exhibit 2.4). To improve product quality, they have introduced teamwork, frequent training, and state-of-the-art logistics. To cut costs, companies have invested in new capital equipment, eliminated unprofitable product and business lines, downsized middle management, and merged with competitors. This is especially the case for companies in the industries that are at the forefront of globalization, such as telecommunications, semiconductors, automobiles, and banking, where megamergers like those between Chrysler and Mercedes and Citibank and Travelers parallel the first wave of mergers at the turn of the century.[27]

Yet as today's globalization entered its next stage, characterized by a Schumpeterian regime of the constructive destruction of industries, operational effectiveness and the managerial revolution that

Exhibit 2.4
Business Strategies for Today's Global Economy: From the 1970s to the 1990s

	Managerial Strategies	Entrepreneurial Strategies
The 1970s	Very Important	Important
The 1990s	Important	Very Important

drove it had already had their place in history and were no longer a sufficient source of competitive advantage. Many of the principles behind the operational effectiveness strategies of TQC, TQM, and reengineering have been broadly diffused throughout the global economy. They have become standard practices. Besides, in saturated markets or in markets where products have already been turned obsolete by new technology or by the competition, a strategy of cost cutting or quality improvements is insufficient. In this sense, though still necessary, strategies that promote operational effectiveness are not sufficient to create sustainable competitive advantages.

To survive and prosper in this new environment, corporations are undergoing a second revolution, an entrepreneurial revolution (see Exhibit 2.4). Under a new set of entrepreneurial strategies known as "strategic alliances," "corporate alliances," and "business networks," corporations are searching for new business opportunities to replace their conventional businesses that have either become the target of imitation or turned obsolete altogether. In fact, companies like Microsoft, Oracle, and America Online have managed to escape price destruction and prosper, precisely because of their ability to shift the focus of their strategy from their managerial functions to their entrepreneurial functions.

As discussed in Chapter 1, transferring the constructive destruction from outside to inside the corporation and shifting the focus of business strategy from the managerial entrepreneurial function of the firm is easier said than done, especially in large corporations. One problem of transferring the constructive destruction from outside to inside the corporation is the friction it creates between winners, those who benefit from the creation of new businesses, and losers, those who lose because of the destruction of the old business. Another problem with turning a large corporation into an entrepreneurial entity is the loosening up of internal controls and hierarchies and the creation of a liberal chaos-like environment conducive to creativity. The creation of such an environment is inconsistent with organizational order and hierarchy. Liberal organizational environments unleash centrifugal forces that may lead to waste of resources and may even threaten the order and cohesion of the organization. A third problem concerning the development of new businesses and products is the integration of technical and market information scattered both inside and outside the corporate organization in marketing departments, distribution centers, suppliers, and even competitors. This is particularly the case for the development and production of complex intelligence-intensive products such as computer software, pharmaceuticals, and multimedia that require market and technical information.

How can such corporations survive the constructive destruction of their businesses? How can they balance concentric forces that pull their organization toward structure and order and centrifugal forces that pull their organization toward chaos and disorder? How can companies integrate market and technical information for the production of complex products? These are questions to be addressed in more detail in subsequent chapters.

NOTES

1. John Bates Clark, *Essentials of Economic Theory* (London: Macmillan, 1907), 533–534.
2. Veblen, 1923, pp. 98–99.
3. Snyder, 1940, p. 8.
4. Dobb, 1958, p. 28.
5. Greenspan, 1998, p. 419.
6. During this period, the world economy was a market fractured by national and local trade barriers rather than a single integrated market. For more details, see Arayama and Mourdoukoutas, 1999a.
7. Veblen, 1923, p. 99.
8. Pusateri, 1984, p. 16.
9. D'Aveni, 1994, p. xiii.
10. Ip, 1998, p. c1.
11. Andrew Osterland and Gary Williams, "From Oil to Gold, It's Down," *Business Week*, 1 June 1998, p. 44.
12. Andrew E. Serwer, "How to Escape a Price War," *Fortune*, 13 June 1994, pp. 82–90.
13. Peter Elsoton, "Let the Telecom Dogfight Begin," *Business Week*, 7 April 1997; Editorial, "The Future of Telecommunications," *Yomiuri Sinbun*, 25 May 1997, p. 3.
14. "Global Crisis" (editorial), *Business Week*, 28 September 1997.

15. Survey, *The Economist*, 20 June 1998, pp. 19–23.

16. David Kilburn, "Japan's Slash to Sell," *Management Today*, January 1996, 52–54.

17. For a detail discussion, see Arayama and Mourdoukoutas, 1999a.

18. Craig Smith and Karry Legget, "China Exporters Fret over High-Priced Yuan," *The Wall Steet Journal*, 7 July 1998, p. A11.

19. Levenstein, 1995, p. 607.

20. Ibid., p. 581.

21. Day, 1908, p. 132.

22. *The Wall Street Journal*, Internet Survey, 8 September 1998, p. 6.

23. Siwolop, 1998, p. BU 5.

24. T. Aeppel, "Keeping the Customer Satisfied," *The Wall Street Journal*, 8 September 1998, p. B4.

25. Editorial, "The Power to Raise Prices," *Business Week*, 4 May 1998, p. 37–39.

26. "Editorial," *The Wall Street Journal*, 2 March 1988.

27. In 1898, for instance, a number of large companies such as National Biscuits were formed as a result of mergers among former competitors. In 1902, U.S. Steel and International Harvester were also formed as a result of mergers and acquisitions. In all, over 2,600 corporations either merged or were acquired by others, with 1,200 disappearing in 1899 alone. For more details, see Pusateri, 1984, p. 200.

_____

Chapter 3

The Limits of Reengineering
and Operational Effectiveness

> All the barbecuing of corporations because of downsizing misses an important point. We see this re-engineering as graphic evidence that the old principles no longer work in the new age.
> —Bruce A. Pasternack and Albert J. Viscio

> The danger in re-engineering, however, is that it merely reinforces the top-down, hierarchical, organizational model of the past century while masquerading as a revolutionary change. It isn't revolutionary, and it isn't the kind of change that will ultimately best serve these corporations.
> —Harry S. Dent, Jr.

For almost a century, work in large hierarchical corporations was organized under Adam Smith's principles of the division of labor. Popularized by Frederick Taylor in the Ford assembly lines, this system of "scientific management" is about a preset, assembly-style production process of standard products like Ford's Model T. In such a production process, which draws a clear line between management and labor, work is divided by an elitist and authoritarian management into simple tasks and assigned to individual workers under a fixed wage. "The managers assume, for instance, the burden of gathering together all of the traditional knowledge by the workmen and then of classifying, tabulating and reducing this knowledge to rules, laws, and formulae which are immensely helpful to the workmen in doing their daily work." In this way, management masters the entire process and labor masters individual tasks, which is the essence of scientific management: "Perhaps, the most important single element in modern scientific management is the task idea. The work of every workman is fully planned out by management at least one day in advance, and each man receives in most cases complete written instructions, describing in detail the task which he is to accomplish, as well as the means to be used in doing the work."[1] Indeed, "individual departments or shops continued to be operated by foremen who were generalists and were on the line of authority and responsibility that ran from the president through the works manager and his direct subordinates."[2]

Is it possible for managers to gather all market and production information, plan production schedules, and supervise labor at the same time? Ford's early success as well as the success of the American machinery industry in the first half of the twentieth century attest to an affirmative answer to this question.[3] Yet, as discussed, this period was an era of fractured markets and sanctuaries, a time when companies competed more against consumers and less against each other. Moreover, this was a period of low saturation and relatively slow technological expansion that made production a fixed process that allowed corporations to mass produce standard products, such as automobiles, household appliances, and industrial engineering. In this sense, it is hard to determine whether the success of the U.S. automobile and machinery industries over this period can be attributed to the division of labor alone. What happened in the second half of the century, when globalization resumed its course, eliminating market sanctuaries and turning producers against producers rather than against consumers?

In such a regime, Adam Smith's principles and Taylor's scientific management that exemplified them became obsolete. As the founders of reengineering, Hammer and Champy argue, "It is no longer necessary or desirable for companies to organize themselves around Adam Smith's division of labor. Task-oriented jobs in today's world of customers' competition and change are obsolete."[4] Globalization has shifted consumer demand from mass-made products to custom-made products, while new technology has shifted production from preset assembly lines that deliver standard products to flexible, programmable assembly lines that deliver custom-made products. Moreover, globalization and new technology have shifted the focus of business enterprise from the narrow concepts of production and mass manufacturing to the broad concept of product supply chain that includes a collection of operations from production to marketing, distribution, and retailing.

Adapting to the new regime, the large corporations of the late 1990s are no longer organized under Adam Smith's principles of the division of labor. Instead, they are organized under a new set of principles that emphasize the allocation of labor by process rather than by individual tasks. Popularized by TQC in Japan, TQM in the United States, and reengineering literature, this new system of organization replaces elitist and authoritarian management with worker teams that are assigned to the entire production process rather than individual tasks. Individual workers rotate from task to task, work closely with each other in teams with little or no supervision from management, and are paid by performance rather than in fixed wages. In this way, workers become masters of the entire production process rather than individual tasks and are accountable for the outcome of the entire process rather than the outcome of a single task. This in turn allows companies to be more responsive to market conditions and to achieve operational effectiveness (i.e., to cut costs, improving product quality at the same time).

In spite of its success, is it possible for corporations to create sustainable competitive advantages based on operational effectiveness alone in a globalizing economy? The answer to this question is negative, for a number of reasons. Logistics and managerial practices that are at the core of reengineering strategies become more expensive and more complicated for companies to adopt and to adapt to, they are easy to imitate, they become less and less effective in competing in saturated markets with a high degree of product obsoleteness, and they are not sufficient for the development of complex products.

Addressing these limitations of reengineering in more detail, this chapter is in five sections. The first section discusses the limitations corporations face in adopting reengineering methods and in adapting their organization to the changes that follow. The second section discusses the problems associated with the imitation of reengineering practices by the competition. The third section discusses the problems associated with the application of reengineering principles in highly saturated markets. The fourth section discusses the problems of applying reengineering in the face of product and business obsoleteness, and the fifth section discusses the issue of product complexity.

ADOPTION AND ADAPTATION

Ever since business enterprises began to rely on the introduction of new technology and managerial practices as competitive vehicles, they have encountered a dual problem. The first part of the problem is the rationalization of the new systems vis-à-vis the old systems that are to be replaced. To be more specific, the costs and benefits of the new systems must be compared and contrasted against the costs and benefits of the old systems. The costs and benefits of a voice mail switchboard, for instance, must be compared and contrasted with the cost of the old manual switchboard system it replaces. This means that technological and managerial systems that are often rationalized and justified on technical grounds may not necessarily be justified on economic grounds. And this could explain why certain technologies that were discovered centuries before the Industrial Revolution never found their way into production of goods and services. The twelfth century in China, for instance, saw a number of technological inventions that never spread over to the production of goods and services because their cost outweighed the cost of abundant inexpensive labor, and because of the radical changes they would bring to the status quo, which leads to the second part of the problem, the adaptation of the organization to the changes brought by the new systems.[5]

New technology and managerial practices are often agents of change, as they alter the ways companies are organized and conduct their internal and external affairs, creating winners and losers. New technology, for instance, creates new business opportunities, and, therefore, it is a source of profits for stockholders and a source of income and employment for workers who work in the new businesses. At the same time, new technology replaces labor and substitutes old sources of supply and distribution channels with new ones, creating losers among the corporation's suppliers, distributors, and workers. New managerial practices eliminate managerial positions, creating winners and losers among the middle and lower management ranks. In this way, new technology and managerial practices create organizational inertia that may diminish or even reverse the positive impact such technology may have on the organization.

Reengineering is no exception to this rule. As discussed earlier, reengineering is about advanced logistics and managerial practices that transform the way corporations perform their basic functions to become efficient and effective. But such a transformation comes at a cost that must be weighed against traditional alternatives before it is adopted. Specifically, logistics come in the form of mathematical models, statistical techniques, and databases that require the purchase and installation of the appropriate hardware and software that can cost companies from a few thousand to hundreds of thousands of dollars and can take several months to install. Oracle Corporation, for instance, charges companies up to $25 million for the installation of the hardware and the software to run relational databases, and they take up to eighteen months to be in full operation. According to statistics by the Computer Reseller and the Gallup Organization published in *The Wall Street Journal* in 1996, large American companies spent, on average, over $2 million on computer networking equipment, medium companies spent $333 thousand, and small companies spent $151 thousand.[6] Worse, as another survey indicates, 31.5 percent of companies overran their budget by 21 to 50 percent, while another 29.9 percent overran their budget by 51 to 100 percent.[7]

Managerial practices such as teamwork and job rotation are not acquired for free either. They are normally taught in-house by consultants and that costs both instructional time and materials and forgone earnings for the employees that attend them. According to some estimates, a day at a training school can cost about $225 per student, while a nine-month training course can reach $6,900.[8] In 1996, American corporations spent close to $2 billion on knowledge management consultants and another $55.3 billion for formal training.[9]

The problem of adopting new technology becomes even more serious as business logistics turn more complex and companies find it increasingly difficult to adopt their parameters and to train their members accordingly. Worse, in an attempt to keep up with competition, companies end up installing technology that they cannot handle. Bernard Wysocki Jr. calls it, "A fast-changing landscape, an increasingly complex array of software, and technology boosters' can-do mentality, even when they can't."[10] In this sense, logistics often turn into a source of inefficiency rather than efficiency and cost the company millions of dollars in losses, damaging its reputation at the same time.

Huron Malune Products is a case in point. The company's early attempts to introduce sophisticated flexible manufacturing and computer-aided design systems failed because they were too sophisticated for its employees. HMO provider Oxford Health Plans is another case in point. The company's inability to train its personnel to new software threw its organization into chaos, resulting in thousands of unpaid bills and losses and hurting the company's relations with its clients and regulators. Pacific Gas & Electric Company is a third case. After spending millions of dollars to introduce a new software from IBM that handled its billing process, the company decided to abandon the software altogether because it did not perform as expected.[11] Huron Malune Products, Oxford Health Plans, and Pacific Gas & Electric Company are not the only companies having trouble adapting their organizations to the demands of advanced logistics. According to a Standish Group International survey, 40 percent of information systems failed in 1996, compared to 31.1 percent in 1994.[12]

If companies find it difficult to introduce new software, they find it even more difficult to keep up with upgrades while their members still strive to familiarize themselves with previous upgrades. Indeed, in a survey published in *The Wall Street Journal*, companies indicated that they are less eager to upgrade their systems to new software from Microsoft. The proportion of home PC users who upgraded their

Windows 3.1 software dropped from 40 percent in January 1996 to 33 percent in January 1997 and 22 percent in January 1998.[13] Similar trends are observed in the business software upgrades, where "part of the backlash comes from a new generation of computer-savvy senior executives . . . who just refuse to spend millions of dollars on bells and whistles that add complexity to systems already prone to breakdown."[14]

Another part of backlash comes from the second problem of introducing logistics and managerial practices; that is, from the changes those logistics and managerial practices bring to the corporate organization. Specifically, some corporations have used reengineering as a scapegoat for the elimination of middle management positions and either lay off redundant managers or transfer them to less-paying jobs. Some companies have advanced even further, with massive layoffs of redundant workers which have demoralized those left behind. In addition, companies must overcome the organizational inertia associated with the nurturing and operation of teams. One problem is the difficulty in getting people to work together as a team rather than as individuals. This is particularly the case in individualistic societies where people are used to working and being rewarded individually. Another problem is the difficulty some corporations have in recruiting people with good analytical and comprehension skills. This is particularly the case in countries where literacy rates are low.

In short, as logistics that are at the core of reengineering become more expensive and more complicated, it becomes more difficult for corporations to rationalize their adoption and to adapt to the changes they bring to the organization. In addition, some reengineering principles, like teamwork, may not be compatible with the individualistic values of certain societies. Besides, as many reengineering practices become universal, reengineering corporations must be concerned with imitation by the competition.

IMITATION

"Human beings have an innate tendency to imitate one another," argued ancient Greek philosophers, a tendency that applies to business managers and strategists who tend to imitate the production methods, logistics, organizational forms, and strategies and practices of their competitors. In fact, the history of capitalism is full of stories of corporations imitating the technology, the management systems, and the competitive strategies of each other. In the last quarter of the nineteenth century, for instance, American entrepreneurs like Francis Lowell and Andrew Carnegie traveled to Great Britain to learn about the ways the British processed steel and cotton, which they replicated back home. In the 1920s, European entrepreneurs traveled to the United States to learn about American technologies and the American system of management, which in turn transferred back to their own corporations. In fact, European entrepreneurs not only emulated the American technology and management systems, they also emulated regulation. As Michael J. Piore and Charles F. Sabel observe, "In the process, they borrowed not only specific components from U.S. industrial technology, but also numerous features of American regulatory institutions. As a result, the economic structures of the major industrial countries come to exhibit a broad family resemblance."[15]

In the late 1940s and the 1950s, American management gurus like W. Edwards Deming traveled to Japan to teach Japanese manufacturers the American system of management and Japanese managers even traveled to the United States to acquire hands-on experience in the American system of management. Paradoxically, after the Japanese studied the American system of scientific management, they abandoned many of its principles, especially the division of labor by individual task. Instead, they came up with their own version, a model of production based on the division of labor by process rather than on the division of labor by task. Dating back to the days of Taiichi Ohno and Eiji Toyoda at Toyota in the 1950s, this model reorganized workers by teams and delegated them the authority to make the day-to-day decisions on each shop floor. Teams held regular meetings to discuss shop problems, and consulted frequently with engineers to find ways to solve those problems and to improve product quality, and that is where the concept of "quality circles," and "continued improvement" came from that eventually turned Japanese companies into formidable competitors for their U.S. counterparts.

If history is full of examples of imitation, things are more so nowadays in the "cyber economy," where information travels instantly through the information highways. This is especially the case for logistics that are based on hardware and software technologies that can be purchased in the market or mathematical models that can be taught in-house by consultants or in MBA schools. A number of well-known logistics, such as inventory control, linear programming, data envelopment analysis, and queuing models, for instance, are taught in every MBA program and come in easy-to-use software packages. The same applies to well-known managerial practices, such as working teams and job rotation, that can be tailored to a company's specifications by scores of consultants.

Thanks to a cottage industry of business consultants, most reengineering practices have become standard practices around the world. Take the *just-in-time* inventory system, teamwork, and job rotation, for instance. In the early 1980s, American and European automobile companies began to introduce these methods to their assembly lines. By the early 1990s, these methods had not only become standard practices for the world automobile industry; they had spread to every major industry around the world. In this sense, operational effectiveness based on logistics and management practices is subject to a serious limitation. As logistics equipment can be purchased in the market, and as many managerial practices can be transferred from one company to another, a competitive strategy based on such factors alone cannot be sustainable over the long term:

Hardware technologies certainly are transferable across companies. Information and telecommunication networks can be purchased in the market and installed in every company. In fact, the use of hardware technology in internal and external communications is no longer an option but a requirement for competing in a global economy. The same is true for software technologies that are also transferable across companies. Training programs, team production, and job rotation, for instance have become standard practices in every company around the world.[16]

The erosion of the competitive advantage of Japanese semiconductor and computer industries in the 1990s is a case in point. Japanese companies that based their strategies on standard logistics and management practices eventually lost their competitive edge to their American counterparts. The Sears catalogue business is another case in point. When Sears started catalogue shopping a few decades ago, it was a pioneering move. But it was not too long before the catalogue business became too crowded, forcing Sears to give up this business altogether. The large U.S. memory chipmaker Micron Technology is a third case in point. Through mass production, Micron Technology initially managed to gain the competitive edge in supplying memory chips to computer makers. Yet before long Asian producers like Samsung Electronics caught up with Micron Technology, flooding the market with low-priced computer memory chips and eliminating Micron Technology's competitive advantage.

Another way companies can pursue operational effectiveness is through mergers between former competitors that create a larger organization, allowing them to take advantage of economies of scale and to survive price wars. The merger between Chase and Chemical banks in the mid-1990s was a case in point. By merging divisions and eliminating duplication, the two companies eliminated 12,500 jobs. But again, such a strategy sets an industry precedent that will soon be followed by the competition. A merger of two companies will be followed by the merger of two other companies, and so on until either a price war or government regulation of the industry become imminent. The experience of U.S. retailers Caldor and Kmart is a case in point. Their strategy focused on developing or acquiring many large stores so the average cost of shelving a product could be below that of the competition. Yet in a few years competitors caught up with them and they both barely escaped bankruptcies in 1995.

The universality of such practices means that reengineering has become a victim of its own success. The more universal such practices become, the less they can serve as a source of sustainable competitive advantage. If every automobile company uses robots in its assembly lines and logistical techniques such as the *just-in-time* inventory system, they can no longer warrant a competitor a sustainable advantage over another. Similarly, if every company applies managerial practices such as teamwork and job rotation, they cannot warrant a sustainable advantage to one competitor over another either, a problem that in developed countries is magnified by market saturation.

SATURATION

Capitalism is, among other things, a system of sharp contrasts. Poverty and wealth can coexist side by side. Some people die because of eating too little, while others die because of eating too much. Some societies live below poverty levels, unable to satisfy their basic needs, while other societies live beyond saturation of their basic needs. In fact, for the developed countries, the saturation of industrial markets and the abundance of goods are "the most consequential and long-term postwar development,"[17] an issue addressed in John Kenneth Galbraith's first edition of *The Affluent Society*, and in *The New Industrial State* more than two decades ago:

Now goods are comparatively abundant. Although there is much malnutrition in the world, more people die in the United States of too much food than of too little. No one suggests that all the steel going into our larger automobiles is of prime urgency. Their size, in fact, is now deplored. For many women and some men, clothing has ceased to be related to protection from exposure and has become, like plumage, almost exclusively erotic.[18]

In developed countries like the United States, Galbraith argued, the problem is not so much in production, in the ability of producers to produce sufficient quantities to accommodate consumer demand, but in their ability to find consumers for their products, an issue further addressed in Baran and Sweezy's *Monopoly Capital*. The authors claim that underconsumption is an inherent problem of capitalism, a problem that has given rise to legions of marketers that try to convince consumers the merits of the one product over another, and even create "artificial" needs: "Price competition has largely receded as a means of attracting the public's custom, and has yielded to new ways of sales promotion: advertising, variation of the products' appearance and packaging, 'planned obsolesence,' model changes, credit schemes, and the like."[19]

If oversupply or underconsumption was a problem three decades ago, it is even more of a problem today. Households are already filled with several models of TVs, VCRs, cameras, and computers, and consumers have been saturated with scores of models that add little or no value to the ones they already possess. According to statistics from International Data Corporation, in 1998, 100 percent of American households owned TVs; 15 percent owned one TV, 31 percent owned two TVs, 26 percent owned three TVs, 16 percent owned four TVs, and 11 percent five or more TVs. Close to 70 percent of American households have subscribed to cable TV, while close to 50 percent of households owned at least one PC.[20]

Once again, reengineering and operational effectiveness are victims of their own success. As corporations become more efficient and effective in producing commodities, they find it increasingly difficult to find buyers for their products without cutting prices and squeezing profit margins. If VCR and PC prices, for instance, fall faster than costs, or if consumers have reached saturation for these products, companies can no longer survive, thrive, and prosper just by lowering costs or by improving product quality, a problem compounded by obsoleteness.

OBSOLETENESS

In the early days of industrialization, commodities turned obsolete when they were all worn out and had no more use value for their owners. In today's global economy, commodities often turn obsolete well before they are worn out and even if they have some use value left for the consumers. This means that the economic value of certain commodities is far below their physical value. This is especially the case for high-technology products, which are quickly made obsolete by new, more-advanced products. In the computer hardware and software industries, for instance, product cycles are as short as six months. This is also the case in wireless communications, where cellular phones and modems replace beepers. This means that what used to be known as durable goods begin to look more and more like fresh fruits and vegetables whose value falls rapidly for every extra day they stay on the shelves. Indeed, according to data published in *The New York Times* in 1998, computer prices were falling by 1 percent weekly. Likewise, the price of computer game software can drop by 1 percent daily.[21]

Obsoleteness is not confined to products. It extends to services, especially those that can be replaced by the Internet. As discussed in Chapter 2, globalization and the spread of the information technology that supports and reinforces it turn conventional products and services obsolete altogether. Shopping on the Internet, for instance, quickly substitutes for conventional shopping, Internet investing substitutes for conventional brokerage investing, and websites substitute for travel agencies, bookstores, flower shops, car dealerships, real estate agencies, and so on.

As products and services turn obsolete at ever faster rates, it becomes increasingly difficult for corporations to recover the cost of their investments. As Eliot Janeway puts it, "It is axiomatic that new technology eats capital faster than capital invested in the old technology can earn its keep. Capitalism has proved more vulnerable to the shortened life of investment than to the falling rate of profit that Marx emphasized."[22] In addition, it becomes more difficult for corporations to strike a balance between prompt delivery and low inventory levels.

Under such conditions, not only does operational effectiveness in production have little relevance as a competitive strategy, but the entire concept of the division of labor by process becomes less relevant. To be more specific, the ever-accelerating pace of product obsoleteness has shifted the focus of business strategy from the division of labor by process and operational effectiveness to the division of entrepreneurship, an issue to be further addressed in Chapter 6.

PRODUCT COMPLEXITY

Developed as an alternative to the conventional concept of the division of labor, reengineering emphasizes the management of economic resources rather than the development of new products, especially the development of complex products.

As discussed in Chapter 2, the development and manufacturing of goods and services in today's global economy is a far more complicated operation than that of the previous periods of capitalism. This is especially the case for high-technology products that require the integration of technical and market information scattered both inside and outside corporate borders. For such projects, the ability to develop complex models lags behind the complexity of the real world. As Arthur M. Schneiderman observed:

Our ability to form mental models of complex situations, however, has not kept pace with the rate of increase in complexity. We have had to devise project planning systems to coordinate the many tasks associated with complex logistical efforts. Building a modern skyscraper or putting a man on the moon requires coordination of the activities of many people and organizations. The division of labor involved in these types of projects is made possible by the ability to specify fully the timing and required interactions among various players.[23]

Once again, the development of such projects dictates new organizational forms that provide the incentives, the communication, and the decision-making mechanisms to accommodate the integration of market and technical information for the discovery and exploitation of new business opportunities. In this sense, competitive strategy is no longer just a managerial issue or a change in the way the production process is organized. It is an entrepreneurial issue. It is about the constructive destruction of the entire corporation and about management of change, processes that require a new approach to the concept of corporation altogether.

In short, as was the case with its predecessor, "scientific management," reengineering has run into a number of limitations, ranging from problems of adoption and adaptation to problems of imitation, market saturation, and product complexity. Such problems have turned reengineering into a business strategy of the past and not a strategy for the future that takes a totally new approach to the concept of business strategy and business organization. What is beyond reengineering?

NOTES

1. Taylor, 1970, p. 9–10.
2. Otto Mayr and Robert C. Post, *Yankee Enterprise* (Washington, D.C.: Smithsonian Institution, 1981), p. 159.
3. Ibid., p. 169.
4. Hammer and Champy, 1993, p. 28.
5. For details, see Arayama and Mourdoukoutas, 1999a.
6. *The Wall Street Journal*, 18 November 1996, p. A2.
7. Bulkeley, 1996, p. R25.
8. Mindell, 1998.
9. Bulkeley, 1996, p. R25.
10. Wysocki, 1998a, p. A1.
11. Ibid.
12. Bulkeley, 1996, p. R25.
13. Clark, 1998, p. B1.
14. Wysocki, 1998a, p. A1.
15. Piore and Sabel, 1984, pp. 133–134.
16. Mourdoukoutas and Papadimitriou, 1998, p. 229.
17. Piore and Sabel, 1984, p. 184.
18. Galbraith, 1984, p. 102.
19. Baran and Sweezy, 1966, p. 115.
20. *Investor's Business Daily*, 13 October 1998, p. A10.
21. Rifkin, 1998, p. 51.
22. Janeway, 1989, p. 48.
23. Schneiderman, 1998, p. 45.

PART II

Beyond Reengineering: Constructive Destruction, Collective Entrepreneurship, and Communities of Common Fate

As globalization continues to gain momentum, the world economy is coming under a super-Schumpeterian regime of perpetual destruction and creation of industries and markets. To compete efficiently and effectively under the new regime, management should pursue a business strategy that transfers constructive destruction from the industry to the company level, a strategy that turns conventional hierarchical corporations into collective entrepreneurships and communities of common fate, a strategy that is based on the principle of the division of entrepreneurship rather than the division of labor.

Chapter 4

The Constructive Destruction of the Corporation

The only sustainable competitive advantage today is the ability to change, adapt and evolve—and do it better than the competition.
—John Marrioti

Change is far more radical than we are at first inclined to suppose.
—Henry Bergson

Though referring to biological systems, Bergson's assertion can be applied to social systems as well, especially in a globalizing economy where change has been far more radical than conventional wisdom inclines to suppose. If corporations are to survive and succeed in such an environment, they "should strike out on new paths rather than travel the worn paths of accepted success," to use John D. Rockefeller's words. And as the following three examples demonstrate, looking beyond the conventional wisdom, "striking out on new paths," can be rewarding for corporations and their stockholders.

- "Computers are too complicated to be sold over the phone or over the Internet," goes the conventional wisdom. The phenomenal success of direct computer seller Dell Computer proved that computers could, indeed, be sold over the telephone or the Internet, setting a new computer distribution trend.

- "Books cannot be sold over the Internet either," goes the conventional wisdom. The success of virtual bookstore Amazon.com proved the conventional wisdom once again wrong. Books could, indeed, be sold over the Internet.

- "Americans are too busy and too ignorant to make improvements to their homes." Building material supplier Home Depot proved the conventional wisdom wrong again. Americans are neither too busy nor too ignorant to improve their homes.

Though isolated, all three examples take business strategy beyond operational effectiveness and reengineering to revenue growth through the constructive destruction of conventional business (i.e., the destruction of an established business and its replacement by new ones): the destruction of the conventional computer store where computer-illiterate customers are browsing different models and lectured by salespersons on the merits and the demerits of different models and its replacement with the virtual computer store where computers can be made to order; the destruction of the conventional bookstore where customers browse around titles and its replacement with the virtual bookstore where books can be purchased at a mouse click; the destruction of the conventional home-improvement industry where homeowners had professionals improve their homes and its substitution with scores of self-helpers who make their own home improvements with materials and advice from building-material suppliers like Home Depot.

In all three cases, industry outsiders, new startups, pursued the strategy of constructive destruction. What if well-established corporations pursued the same strategy? As discussed briefly in previous chapters, such a strategy will create friction between winners and losers and will fuel concentric forces pulling the organization toward order and conformity and centrifugal forces pulling the organization toward disorder and creativity. A strategy of constructive destruction will further require the integration of market and technical information scattered both inside and outside the corporation for the discovery and exploitation of new business opportunities to replace the old ones. In other words, the success or failure of a strategy of constructive destruction depends on how skillfully management masters the friction between winners and losers, balances concentric and centrifugal forces, and integrates market and technical information.

Addressing these issues in more detail, this chapter has four sections. The first section discusses constructive destruction as business strategy, while the subsequent sections discuss the conditions for successfully carrying out such a strategy, namely, the minimization of friction between winners, the balancing of concentric and centrifugal forces, and the integration of market and technical information.

CONSTRUCTIVE DESTRUCTION AS BUSINESS STRATEGY

Constructive destruction of businesses and industries is not a new phenomenon in the history of capitalism. As Karl Marx and Joseph Schumpeter and their disciples have argued, the destruction of established industries and their replacement by new ones is in the very nature of capitalism, a system where private capital is in perpetual search for new profit opportunities. Capital flows out of established industries where competition and market saturation have narrowed profit opportunities into new industries where new technology, international trade, demographic trends, and consumer preferences have expanded profit opportunities. In preindustrial capitalism, for instance, capital flowed out from crowded European markets to the emerging markets of colonies. In the industrial capitalism of the nineteenth century, capital continued to flow to the emerging markets of colonies and to new industries created by the spread of steam and electric technologies.

In recent years capital has been flowing to the emerging markets of the former socialist countries and to industries previously under control of the government or government-owned monopolies, such as telecommunications, utilities, and transportation. Capital has also been flowing out of industries that served the younger generations to industries which serve the older generations, and is pouring into biotechnology and computer and software technologies. But where does capital flow from here? Where are profit opportunities to be found in the future?

Certainly, capital will continue to chase after demographic trends for new profit opportunities in the health and leisure industries that serve the needs of an aging population. Capital will also take advantage of new technologies to deliver entirely new products and services to consumers. Yet for some products it is clear that world markets have already reached saturation, and as capitalism approaches its geographical frontiers, it will become increasingly difficult for capital to exploit new market frontiers in faraway markets, as was the case with earlier globalization. Neither will it find former socialist countries or government-protected industries to exploit, as has been the case in recent years. Besides, some former socialist countries may never create the physical and legal infrastructure conducive to capitalist development.

The opportunities of the future are to be found in the perpetual and prompt discovery and exploitation of new products and businesses that compete directly against established businesses, often provided by the same company: the replacement of the telephone pager with the cellular phone; the replacement of conventional telephone calling with internet calling; the replacement of conventional cameras with digital cameras; and the replacement of an old surgical stent device with a new one. This means that in the future capitalism will turn into a "wild cannibal." It will undermine its own markets by turning businesses and products obsolete at ever faster rates; it will transfer the constructive destruction of business from the industry level to the company level; it will turn companies into "mini-cannibals" that take apart their own business. AT&T is a case in point. In 1998, to fend off competition from "dial around" upstarts that let telephone subscribers get around their telephone carriers, the company began its own upstart Lucky Dog Telephone Company. Though the new company may help AT&T regain some of its customers, it may also cannibalize AT&T's existing telephone markets (i.e., it may lure some of its regular subscribers from the traditional calling services to "dial around" services). As Mehta puts it, "With its new effort, AT&T risks channeling its own high-paying customers into a lower-priced option."[1] Home Depot is another case in point. In 1998, the company began working together with contractors to directly enter the home-improvement market, undermining its conventional pioneering do-it-yourself business.

In this sense, the transfer of constructive destruction from the industry level to the corporate level means that corporations must continuously review and restructure their business portfolio, reallocating resources from declining to expanding businesses by leveraging their capabilities. Japan watchmaker Citizen Watch is a case in point.[2] In the last ten years, the company's business was to apply its watch-making capabilities to the development of a broad array of precision instruments that have been slowly replacing its declining product lines. IBM is another case in point. By leveraging its hardware capabilities, the company shifted its focus from computer mainframe manufacturing, a capital-intensive and highly competitive market segment, to services, a strategy that eventually turned the company around. In 1996, for instance, computer mainframes accounted for about 7 percent and services for about 20 percent of the company's business compared to 17 percent and about 11 percent, respectively, in 1992. In the meantime, IBM's stock soared from below $40 to over $150. Germany's Hoechst is a third case in point. The company leveraged its knowledge and expertise in the traditional chemical manufacturing business to expand to the higher-profit-margin life science business. As the CEO of the company put it in his 1997 annual message to the company shareholders

In view of the dynamic developments in the different markets, we can't maintain leading positions in a number of entirely unrelated business. If we want to sustainably increase shareholder value, then we have to deploy our resources in a targeted way. This is why we intend to focus on life science business and exit from the industrial chemicals sector. In other words Hoechst, as we've known it for decades, will cease to exist. Step-by-step, we are creating a new, forward looking Hoechst.[3]

To be durable, a strategy that leverages a company's capabilities must do more than just shift focus from one product line to another. It should discover and exploit radically new business opportunities, "unleashing the Killer apps," as Larry Daws and Chunka Mui put it, developing products that create mass markets, to "establish a new category and by being first, dominates it, returning several hundred percent return of the capital invested."[4] The case of Johnson & Johnson's introduction of "stent" surgical devices is a case in point. An innovative device in the treatment of coronary diseases, the product established a "new category," of medical devices, and was an "eye-popping bonanza" for its developer and manufacturer, generating over $1 billion in sales in a thirty-seven-month period.[5] Yet unfortunately for Johnson & Johnson, because of internal problems in its cardiac division the company failed to follow through with the next generation of stent devices to match the competition, which was already closing in.

Johnson & Johnson's case reaffirms our earlier points about constructive destruction: It must be prompt and perpetual, and take place in an organizational environment that minimizes the friction between winners and losers, balances the crosscurrents of creativity and innovation with those of conformity, and integrates market and technical information efficiently and effectively.

MINIMIZE FRICTION BETWEEN
WINNERS AND LOSERS

Karl Marx is not popular these days. The system he envisioned failed and collapsed, at least in the form it was pursued in the former socialist countries. Yet Marx's enormous work in the three volumes of *Das Kapital* and in *Grundrise* continues to reveal a dynamic and yet contradictory system, a system in constant fight against itself, a system of perpetual creation and destruction of its own industries. In this sense, "the true barrier to capitalist production is capital itself," as Marx put it, a thesis popularized by Joseph Schumpeter, who argues that "capitalism is by nature a form of method of economic change and not only never is but never can be stationary."

Marx further emphasized that capitalism's dynamism does not benefit the society at large, and that capitalism's striving against itself creates winners and losers and places one social class against another, leading to social unrest that may reverse the benefits from capitalism's dynamism. This is a point further elaborated by Veblen, who also emphasized the contradiction between capitalism's drive for efficiency on the one side and profit on the other. Veblen argued that the abandonment of traditional product and business lines creates redundant resources that cannot be deployed to new business lines overnight. This is especially the case for workers and managers who lack the skills to perform the new tasks required in the newly created product and business lines. In addition, workers who lost their jobs in the old business lines may have to wait quite some time before the new businesses are developed, and they may even be replaced by newly recruited workers in possession of such skills. Worse, new jobs may be created in other locations, which means that displaced employees may have to emigrate to the new locations if they want to stay with the same company. In this sense, constructive destruction of business creates winners and losers and internal friction far more extensive and pervasive than reengineering. And as the history of capitalism confirms, unless properly managed and contained, internal friction threatens to derail the entire process of organizational development and growth. What is the solution?

For Marx, the solution was the replacement of capitalism with socialism; that is, the socialization of the means of production, which in practice means the turning over of factories and offices to government bureaucrats, unions, and to party bosses. Unfortunately for Marx and his followers, socialism of this sort could not and did not work. Not only did socialization of the means of production not minimize the friction between winners and losers, not only did it not spread the benefits of collective production to the society at large, it did not create that many benefits to spread at all. And there were not that many benefits to spread because there was little progress and little dynamism. There was little destruction of old business because there was no innovation. And there was no innovation because government appointed managers had neither the freedom nor the knowledge and the incentives to innovate, and they did not have the broad support of the members of their organization.

If a business strategy of constructive destruction of the capitalist corporation is to be pursued successfully, if the friction between winners and losers is to be minimized, corporations must take two important steps: plan and raise support for change, and spread the risks and the rewards from change.

Plan and Raise Support for Change

In spite of its rapid pace, change in a corporate business environment does not come overnight; it is not an entirely new and unpredictable event. As is often the case with humans, corporations find comfort in the status quo, in the way they have been doing business for years, and become complacent with good times. They believe that good fortunes can last forever and so make little effort to prepare themselves for the bad times. In fact, many corporations rush to change things only after bad times reach home. Change comes at a time of crisis, when corporations "suffer high levels of administrative stress, low levels of trust, a great deal of secretiveness and centralization of power and authority, rigid reliance on past strategies, leading to conservatism and risk aversion, and a high degree of conflict coupled with a low degree of morale."[6]

Coming at such a poor time, change tears corporations apart. Stockholders and workers blame management for bad choices and waste of resources. Management blames workers for being unwilling to pay the price for the necessary adjustments, such as pay cuts or outright layoffs, and stockholders for being shortsighted and interested in short-term profits rather in the long-term growth of the corporation.

In this sense, change is a political issue. It divides the organization into those who are for it and to those who are against it, into those who are for the abandonment of declining business lines and their replacement with expanding business lines, and those with vested interests in the status quo.

Friction and conflict can be minimized if the two sides make the necessary preparations for change and address ahead of time, while the corporation is still in good economic health, the consequences of change and prepare the organization accordingly rather than wait until the crisis comes home. As Constantine Markides puts it, "Established companies that want to strategically innovate must take the time to question the way they do business, especially when they are successful. They should not wait for a crisis to start contemplating the future."[7]

One step in this direction is the continuous training and upgrading of every member of the organization to the demands of new technology. Another step is the continuous deployment of the labor force to many tasks within the company and the company affiliates and partnerships so members develop contextual knowledge that allows them to adapt faster to the changing business environment. A third step is the creation of open communication channels among all organization members, "keeping people up to date with their technical knowledge and for developing their skills as managers and leaders or effective colleagues in highly complex and demanding situations."[8] In this way, organization members can understand the necessity for the changes that are to take place and the ways it will affect their lives. As Bruce A. Pasternack and Albert J. Viscio put it, "The burden is fully on the company to clearly communicate the basis of the employment relationship to all its employees abreast of issues facing the company and the implications for them as individuals," although this process, "does absorb energy in coping with it and unless this is allowed for in on-going plans the problems we thought were going to confront us may turn out not to be the ones that are there in fact, or that the ones that are there are beyond our capabilities."[9] A fourth step is the creation of a shared perception of the need for change, by sharing information and perspectives about the competitive position of the firm and future prospects, an issue to be further addressed in Chapter 6.

In short, the problem corporations have adjusting to change is not change per se, but the failure of management to anticipate and plan change and to raise support for it, an issue closely related to the spread of risks and rewards associated with change.

The Spread of Risks and Rewards

The Chinese have two characters for crisis that is often associated with change; one character means opportunity and the other means danger. For corporations that pursue a strategy of constructive destruction, change is inevitably associated with both opportunity, the chance to raise revenues from the discovery and exploitation of new products and business, and danger, the risk of failure to discover the new business and products, and the risk of losses from the transfer of resources from the old to the new business lines. How can management spread such risks and rewards?

Certainly, there is no magic formula to "fairly" share the risks and rewards, especially in large organizations where it is difficult to monitor and calculate the contribution of each individual member, whether a stockholder, a worker, or a manager, to the performance of the organization. Yet economists and business strategists have come up with a number of ideas and measures and suggestions that to some extent spread the risks and rewards of change. One such measure is the spreading of the risks and benefits from the top down rather than from the bottom up. Specifically, in bad times, top executives should serve as an example by being the first ones to take a pay cut rather than just laying off workers. Japanese companies have been good at that. By contrast, American executives have not followed this rule, especially automobile manufacturers that have been notorious in rewarding their top executives with hefty bonuses even at times they lay off thousands of workers. Another measure is the introduction and extension of a bonus system to the majority or even the entirety of the members of the organization. A third measure is the introduction of Employee Stock Ownership Plans (ESOP) or outright stock option plans that turn the organization into a kind of collective entrepreneurship, an issue to be further addressed in the next chapter.[10] A fourth measure is the creation of a corporate welfare fund that will provide a "safety net" for those who cannot keep up with change and are eventually forced out of the organization. In fact, as capitalism takes more and more responsibilities away from government, it must also provide for the welfare of its employees that fall victim to progress. This does not mean that corporations should be turned into welfare agencies, as was the case with corporations in former socialist countries of Europe and in China, but that they should fill part of the gap created by the scaling back of government intervention into the economy.

The spread of risks and rewards should not be confined just to the corporation's members. It should extend to its alliances and affiliates. In this sense, corporations should function more as communities of common fate rather than simply as profit maximizing enterprises, an issue further discussed in Chapter 6.

In short, to deal with one of the side effects of constructive destruction, the friction between winners and losers, management must plan and raise support for change and must spread the risks and rewards associated with it. In this way, "the inertia of institutions will be less powerful. Negative energy will be less dominant. Individuals within the organization will begin to say, 'Hey, let's try it this way, or Wow, what about this?' The manager will have liberated important change and improvement forces within the organization and decreased resistant forces."[11]

Having liberated important change, management in essence has unleashed centrifugal forces that pull the organization toward disorder and creativity, forces that are in clash with the concentric forces that pull the organization toward order and conformity. How can management balance the two forces?

BALANCE CONCENTRIC AND CENTRIFUGAL FORCES

As discussed in Chapter 3, large hierarchical corporations have for decades been under the legacy of Frederick W. Taylor's system of organization that divided production into single tasks to be performed by individual workers under the close supervision of management. Taylor's system further imposed limits and bounds on individual members' behavior regarding the way they performed their duty to the corporation and their interaction with each other and with management:

The essence of management was to develop the means of control to pattern workers' behavior within the production process. The basis of scientific management was the ordering of work behavior through time and motion studies. . . . The intent was to discover the roles of informal human groups in a formal organization and to maintain equilibrium between formal and informal organizations.[12]

But that was then, at the turn of the century, when organizational order and conformity were synonymous with efficiency and productivity, when production was a fixed process, and when corporations competed with each other on costs. As reengineering theorists demonstrated, Taylor's system is incompatible with today's business world. The division of labor by task and close worker supervision, for instance, are no longer the crucial factors for the competitiveness of a corporation. On the contrary, in many cases those factors are impediments to the efficient operation and competitiveness of a corporation. Strict specialization and close supervision, for instance, discourage individual initiative and creativity. The discovery and exploitation of new businesses, in particular, require a less-structured working environment where employees are free to experiment with new ideas. As Nemeth has put it. "Creativity and innovation may require a 'culture' that is very different and, in a sense, diametrically opposed to that which encourages cohesion, loyalty, and clear norms of appropriate attitudes and behavior."[13]

Reflecting these concerns, Taylor's legacy is gradually fading away. Limits and bounds on individual behavior are stretched out and have become more flexible to allow individual members to experiment with new things and to work under a trial-and-error system with little supervision, rather than under a system of formal rules and procedures and close supervision. In such an organization structure, the "essence of management" is disorder and chaos rather than order and conformity. As Ikujiro Nanaoka observes, "Chaos widens the spectrum of options and forces the organization to seek new points of view. For an organization to renew itself, it must keep itself in a non-equilibrium state at all times."[14] This is especially the case in large established hierarchical corporations where management is detached from stockholders. Sumatra Ghoshal and Christopher A. Barlett write, "Top management's objective must be to reduce reliance on formal control systems and increase self-discipline instead. In a self-disciplined organization, employees come to meetings on time, work toward agreement on defined agendas, and do not question in the corridors the decisions they agreed to in the conference room."[15]

What if self-discipline does not work? What if organization members do not come to meetings on time? What if they use corporate time to pursue an agenda different than that of the organization? In that case, the new organization model would not work, and it would not bear the right results (i.e., the successful development of new products and businesses). But even if the organization members pursue the agenda of the organization and develop new products and businesses, such products and businesses may not accomplish these tasks in a timely and cost effective fashion.

Game software maker Broderbund is a case in point.[16] To foster creativity and innovation, the company adopted a liberal, university-like working environment, where employees could set their own goals and their own pace of work, take their children to work, and take sabbaticals at the company's Creativity Center. "Every employee, for example, could expect regular sabbaticals, lasting two to three months, at the company's Creativity Center to recharge their batteries and work on any idea at all, no matter how far-fetched or uncertain its commercial prospects."[17]

In the beginning, employee freedom to exploit original, breakthrough ideas without concern for their commercial applications bore the right results. Broderbund produced blockbuster games such as *Myst* and *Riven*, and its profit and market capitalization soared. Yet in such a liberal environment, costs became out of control. Characteristically, *Riven* cost more than $10 million to produce, compared to its predecessor *Myst*, which cost only $600 thousand. With costs getting out of control, and with profit margins squeezed by competition, Broderbund eliminated sabbaticals at its Creativity Center and began to set firm deadlines for projects returning to a more traditional organization structure of order and conformity:

The most profound change for veteran Broderbunders was the belt-tightening and cost controls, in effect a dose of old-fashioned, traditional management by the bottom line. The days of flexible budgets and free spending were quickly replaced by a cost consciousness that put every creative decision under scrutiny.[18]

Though an isolated example, the case of Broderbund is not unique. In fact, the problem of balancing concentric and centrifugal forces is more evident in corporations that rush to expand their product lines through acquisitions. In that case, the conservative culture of one company may not blend well with the liberal culture of another company. This is particularly the case when the acquirer is a large hierarchical company, the acquired is a small nonhierarchical company, and the acquisition is hostile. The case of Johnson & Johnson's acquisition of Cordis is a case in point. Cordis's liberal nonhierarchical corporate culture did not blend well with Johnson & Johnson's hierarchical conservative culture. As a result, the acquisition did not fair well, and that was one of the reasons Johnson & Johnson failed to follow through with a new generation of surgical stent devices, as discussed earlier in this chapter.[19]

The cases of Broderbund and Johnson & Johnson reveal the difficulties corporations have in striking a balance between concentric forces that pull the organization toward order and conformity and centrifugal forces that pull the organization toward chaos and creativity. They also reveal the difficulties in striking a balance between organizational structures that promote managerial efficiency and structures that promote entrepreneurial effectiveness. In this sense, the key to successful innovations is a hybrid working environment that "blends limited structure around responsibilities and priorities with extensive communication and design freedom to create improvisation within current projects. This combination is neither so structured that change cannot occur nor so unstructured that chaos ensues."[20] In practice, this means that corporations should put their operations under a dual organization structure. Operations such as financial management should be placed under a centralized conservative structure, while product development should be placed under a decentralized liberal structure.

In short, as corporations begin to shift their focus from narrow business strategies that pursue operational effectiveness to broad strategies that pursue the constructive destruction of their businesses, they must minimize the friction between winners and losers by preparing and raising support for change and spreading the risks and the rewards associated with it. Corporations must be further prepared to deal with crosscurrents of concentric forces pulling the organization toward order and conformity that promote operational effectiveness and centrifugal forces pulling the organization toward disorder and creativity that promote the discovery and exploitation of new businesses:

Managers of excellent companies seek bounded instability, even though they may not be explicitly aware of doing so, because it is vital to success. Instability is not just due to ignorance but rather is a fundamental property of successful business institutions. Successful managers use constrained instability in a way to provoke innovation.[21]

Balancing the two forces is not an easy task, especially when corporations try to integrate market and technical information.

INTEGRATION OF MARKET AND TECHNICAL INFORMATION

In the preindustrial and early industrial eras, the discovery and exploitation of new business opportunities was by and large left to individual entrepreneurs, inventors, financiers, and adventurers who had the ability to gather the technical and market information for the discovery and exploitation of new business opportunities. But as will be discussed in more detail in the next chapter, the preindustrial and early industrial eras were relatively simple worlds compared to the later industrial era, and especially today's post-industrial economy. In mid-nineteenth-century America, for instance, textile mills like the Pepperel mill that employed 800 people at a time, and managers could learn all about the business in a "matter of a few hours."[22] The same was true in the case of the cotton and garment industries, where a single manager was in a position to know all the details about the business.

In the later industrial era, the discovery and exploitation of new business opportunities was left to professional managers and experts, what J. K. Galbraith calls "technostructure." But even the later industrial era was a relatively simple world compared to today's post-industrial era. Managers had to be experts in one area rather in many areas at the same time. Besides, later industrialization was a world of large oligopoly firms too complacent to pursue radically new business opportunities and to assume the risks associated with them.

In today's post-industrial era, the discovery and exploitation of new business opportunities cannot be left either to individual entrepreneurs or professional managers. For all practical purposes, professional managers are too complacent and individuals do not possess all the market and technical information to transfer new technology from the lab to the factories and the offices, turning it into mass-market products. This is especially the case in high-technology industries, such as the Internet, computer hardware, computer software, and cellular phones, industries that are founded on a hybrid of different technologies rather than a single technology.

In such industries, the successful development and launch of new business is a collective (an "organizational capability") issue rather than an individual or professional management capability issue. It is the result of organizational capabilities rather than individual capabilities. As Robert M. Grant observes, "Integration of specialist knowledge to perform a discrete productive task is the essence of *organizational capability*, defined as a firm's ability to perform repeatedly a productive task, which relates either directly or indirectly to a firm's capacity for creating value through effecting the transformation of inputs into outputs."[23] This is often the case even for marginal product improvements and innovations: "Even when the innovation is more than an increase in size or variation on an established theme it is probable that a whole team of specialists will have to be established to pool their resources and share the project."[24] In this sense, "Success will come to those companies that build a knowledge base about their competitive environment and a perpetual strategy process to keep it continuously updated."[25] Conversely, "Without a learning capability, the organization would never have come into being, and if the need to change is ignored for too long, the organization will perish as surely as if it was denied capital, employees, and markets."[26] In this sense, "Failure to create knowledge and manage it as a critical organizational asset may account for the declining performance of well-established firms."[27]

The development of organizational capabilities, in turn, is a matter of integration of market and technical information. Formally

> Technical Information + Market Information
> = Organizational Capabilities.

The development of computer software products, for instance, is the result of the integration of market and technical information scattered across hundreds of engineers and marketers both inside and outside the conventional borders of software corporations. Similarly, the design and development of computer hardware products require the integration of market and technical information that cannot be owned or controlled by one individual alone, or amassed in a research lab of a single corporation.

In most cases, technical information is scattered both inside and outside the corporation, in its own production and research centers, in government laboratories, and even in the laboratories of the company's competitors. Similarly, market information is scattered across private market-research institutions, databases, distribution centers, and retail departments.[28] Some of it is in the form of hard data that can be easily transferred over the information highways but other is in the minds of the very people that work in each center or department. As Victor Fung puts it, "As the sources of supply explode, managing information becomes increasingly complex. Of course, we have a lot of hard data about performance and about work we do with each factory. But what we really want is difficult to pin down; a lot of the most valuable information resides in people's heads."[29] And information can be integrated only if people are willing to communicate and cooperate with each other.

This means that the development of new products is a collective effort, the result of cooperation among several, often competing, corporations. The development of digital displays and high-performance PCs is a case in point. Competing companies such as Compaq, Dell, IBM, NEC, Hewlett Packward, and Fujitsu have joined forces with Intel, Microsoft, and Silicon Image to form a Digital Display Working Group that will set the standards for the developing and manufacturing of the next generation of flat panel displays and high-performance PCs. The development of cellular phone software is also an example. Competing mobile companies Telefor Ericsson, Motorola, and Nokia, for instance, have joined forces with software maker Psion Plc to develop software for their new generation of mobile phones.[30]

The integration of market and technical information takes two things. First, it takes an efficient communication structure (i.e., hardware and software technologies that allow the members of the corporation to communicate efficiently and effectively with each other and with suppliers, customers, and collaborators). As we discussed elsewhere, hardware technologies include the Internet, intranets, groupware, videoconferencing equipment, and any technology that allows a company to build its information network system or to connect with the outside information highways. Software technologies include organizational arrangements such as job rotation, labor transfers, and companywide conferences that allow the members of the organization to develop contextual knowledge (i.e., learn different tasks). Second, it takes the mastery of internal and external relations that turn conventional corporations into entrepreneurial networks and communities of common fate, issues that are further addressed in the next two chapters.

As capitalism is reaching its final frontier, the global economy, companies can no longer compete for distant markets, as was the case in the earlier globalization, and neither can they create market sanctuaries, as was the case in the period between early globalization and today's globalization. Instead, they must compete against themselves by perpetually abandoning their businesses that have either been invaded by competition or turned obsolete altogether and replacing them with entirely new ones.

To pursue such strategies, corporations must address three problems associated with them. Namely, they must minimize the friction between winners and losers, balance concentric and centrifugal forces, and integrate market and technical information for the discovery and exploitation of new business opportunities. In addition, they must turn themselves into collective entrepreneurships and communities of common fate, organizations discussed in the next two chapters.

NOTES

1. Stephanie N. Mehta, "Dog Teaches New Trick to AT&T," *The Wall Street Journal*, 7 October 1998, p. B1.

2. Patton, 1997.

3. Hoechst, 1997 Annual Report, p. 6.

4. Downes, Mui, and Negroponte, 1998, p. 4.

5. Winslow, 1998, pp. A1, A5.

6. Hickman and Silva, 1987, p. 52.

7. Markides, 1998, p. 34.

8. Whitfield, 1975, p. 148.

9. Pasternack and Viscio, 1998, p. 83.

10. To be successful, ESOP and stock option plans must be for real and not in name only. Specifically, true ESOPs must allow the members of the organization to participate in the decision making process, otherwise they may turn into a source of instability rather than a source of stability. The Northwest ESOP plan is a case in point. Failure of management to include labor as partners in the decision-making process turned into a bitter dispute that led to the August 1998 strike. For details, see Leondhardt, 1998.

11. Tropman and Morningstar, 1989, p. 42.

12. Nonaka, 1988, p. 57.

13. Nemeth, 1997, p. 59.

14. Ibid.

15. Ghoshal and Barlett, 1995, p. 91.

16. For a detailed discussion, see Rifkin, 1998, pp. 48–58.

17. Ibid., p. 50.

18. Ibid., p. 53.

19. For further discussion, see Winslow, 1998, p. A5.

20. Brown and Eisenhardt, 1997, p. 1.

21. Stacey, 1992, p. 79.

22. Blackford and Kerr, 1986, p. 113.

23. Grant, 1996, p. 377 (italics added).

24. Whitfield, 1975, p. 122.

25. Tyson, 1998, p. 14.

26. Downes, Mui, and Negroponte, 1998, p. 168.

27. Inkpen, 1996, p. 123.

28. Market information refers to knowledge of demand and supply conditions in various commodity and resource markets, especially knowledge about insufficiently explored resource or commodity markets. For details, see Casson, 1982, p. 67.

29. Magretta, 1998a, p. 112.

30. "Phone Giants Team Up to Challenge Microsoft," *The Wall Street Journal*, 25 June 1998, p. A6.

Chapter 5

The Concept of
Collective Entrepreneurship

> Change must be reducible to an arrangement or rearrangement of
> parts; the irreversibility of time *must* be an appearance relative to
> our ignorance; the inability of man to put things in place again.
> —Henri Bergson

Certainly man cannot turn the clock back and put things the way
they were, but man can arrange and rearrange institutions to adopt
and adapt to change, especially in a rapidly changing global economy,
where, under unprecedented ideological, technological, and economic
forces, institutions mutate into forms never seen before. More and
more companies are lowering their internal barriers that separate their
stockholders from their managers and their managers from their
workers: They delegate decisions from top management to labor
teams, pay bonuses and stock options to the majority of their employees, and emphasize the importance of a sound corporate vision
over direct management controls, turning each and every member
into an entrepreneur. In addition, more and more companies are lowering their external boundaries that separate them from their suppliers, distributors, customers, and their competitors. Producers work
more closely with their suppliers, distributors, and retailers to cut

down delivery time and to reduce inventory costs. Customers work more closely with producers to identify new market trends and to improve product quality. Former competitors work more closely to exploit new business opportunities.

The mutations and permutations of traditional market institutions have created modern fluid market institutions that challenged the traditional concepts of "firm" and "industry." Specifically, with firms competing and cooperating with each other at the same time, they can no longer be defined as hierarchical structures, as distinct and separate entities from other firms. Neither can an industry be defined simply as the sum of individual firms producing a specific product or service and competing with each other. Instead, firms should be defined as collective entrepreneurships, entrepreneurial networks gradually spreading over and replacing traditional hierarchical firms. Likewise, industries should be defined as constellations of entrepreneurial networks engaged in the same activity.

Addressing the formation of new institutions in a globalizing economy, this chapter takes a closer look at the concept of collective entrepreneurship in three sections. The first section discusses the "other" function of the firm, entrepreneurship, the second section compares and contrasts the concepts of individual and collective entrepreneurship throughout the history of capitalism, and the third section discusses different types of collective entrepreneurship.

ENTREPRENEURSHIP: THE OTHER FUNCTION OF THE FIRM

In capitalist economies, firms perform a dual function as managerial and as entrepreneurial units. As managerial units firms are engaged in the management of economic resources (i.e., the allocation of economic resources toward the achievement of certain output, profit, and cost goals). As entrepreneurial units firms are engaged in the discovery and exploitation of new business opportunities (i.e., they bridge the gap between labs, research institutions, and factories and offices that develop new ideas and products and the market where such ideas and products are tested against consumer demands).

For decades, economists by and large have been preoccupied with the managerial rather than the entrepreneurial function of the firm. In fact, mainstream economists view entrepreneurship simply as an abstract category, some kind of magical impersonal risk-taking operation that brings resources together and coordinates production. In fact, the controversy over entrepreneurship almost disappeared by the early 1930s, "just before the complete development of the modern theory of the firm," namely, before the publication of Samuelson's *Foundation of Economic Analysis.*[1] In either case, entrepreneurship is often treated the same as the management and organization of businesses in general.[2]

Economists' bias against entrepreneurship is consistent with both the modern philosophy and the methodology of the discipline. Specifically, mainstream economics is concerned with static operational problems such as the optimal allocation of resources to alternative uses that can be analyzed mathematically rather than dynamic philosophical issues and institutions. As W. J. Baumol observes,

The theory of the firm has based its results almost entirely on the premise of optimization. Firms are taken to hire the profit-maximizing number of workers, to retain optimal quantities of inventory, to apportion their capital optimally among the company's various products—those that constitute its most profitable product line. Mathematicians have provided to economics a set of most powerful tools for the analysis of optimal decisions.[3]

Mark Casson provides two additional explanations about economists' bias toward the managerial function of the firm. First is the assumption of perfect information that places every firm on an equal footing regarding the discovery and exploitation of new business opportunities, an assumption that "reduces decision-making to the mathematical application of mathematical rules of optimization."[4] Second is the difficulty associated with the development of an objective theory of the entrepreneurial function of the firm. In either case, the focus of economics is on the clarity and consistency of mathematical models rather than on their fair and accurate representation of the real world they are assumed to explain.

An exception to the rule is the Austrian school of economics and Joseph Schumpeter in particular, who treats entrepreneurship as a distinct and separate function of the firm: "The function of entrepreneurs is to reform or revolutionize the pattern of production by exploiting an invention or, more generally, an untried technological possibility for producing a new commodity or producing an old one in a new way, by opening up a new source of supply of materials or a new outlet for products, by recognizing an industry and so on."[5] Specifically, Schumpeter identified five ways of "revolutionizing the pattern of production":

- The development of a new product (i.e., a product never introduced before or the substantial improvement of quality of an existing product).
- The discovery of a new production method. The term "discovery" does not necessarily mean scientific discovery but the genuine application of an existing method to an industry.
- The discovery and exploitation of a new market. The term "discovery" does not necessarily apply to a new geographical market or an unknown market, but rather a market that an industry has not expanded before.
- The discovery and exploitation of a new source of supply of raw materials. Again, the term "discovery" does not necessarily apply to a new geographical resource market or an unknown resource, but rather a resource that was never used in a certain industry.
- The introduction of a new organization in a new industry. This means the creation of a market sanctuary like a monopoly or the breaking of a market sanctuary. A new organization further means a new way of manufacturing, assembly, transporting, or delivering a product to customers.

Treating production as a social and dynamic rather than as a technical and static process, Schumpeter developed a theory of corporate renewal and growth with the entrepreneur as an innovator at the center of that process, an approach that gradually gained some followers. Criticizing the philosophical bias and limitations of the operational approach to the theory of the firm, Ludwig von Mises's student, Israel M. Kirzner, for instance, attributes economists' failure to develop an entrepreneurial theory of the firm to the strong belief that central planning rather than markets is the engine of economic growth:

It is therefore hardly surprising to find that this earlier growth and development literature not only failed to explore the policies and institutional patterns that might stimulate profit-motivated individual market-entrepreneurship; it in fact tended to take it for granted that markets were entirely unnecessary for the achievement of growth, and that the naturally preferred mode for growth was through wise central planning.[6]

In view of the failures of central planning, Kirzner argues that economists must expand their theories to include the evaluation of alternative profit opportunities:

Economists can no longer take it for granted that individual decision makers, or groups, engage in nothing more than allocative decisions against the background of clearly perceived alternatives. Economists must consider that economic processes, and especially market processes have profound impact upon the way in which individuals perceive the options available to them, while the accuracy and sensitivity of opportunity-perception itself crucially affects the nature of the economic and market processes that they set in motion. In other words, economic analysis must grapple with the inescapable entrepreneurial element in action and in society.[7]

The bias toward the managerial function of the firm is not confined to economic-theory literature. It extends to business-strategy-theory literature too, and for good reason. The primary function of business strategists is the interpretation and simplification of economists' complex models and the offering of practical advice to managers of large corporations on the allocation and control of economic resources. Popular business strategies, such as TQC, TQM, and reengineering, are the case in point. With all their contentions about radical new ways of organizing businesses, all three theories are just about different ways of allocating resources so corporations can achieve operational effectiveness, rather than ways of exploring new business opportunities. As Hammer and Champy have put it, "We believe that, in general the difference between winning companies and losers is that winning companies know how to do their work better. If American companies want to become winners again, they will have to look to how they get their work done."[8]

But again, there are exceptions to the rule. A substantial part of the business-strategy literature has been devoted to entrepreneurship. A group of business strategists has researched the physiological and the socioeconomic profile of successful entrepreneurs. Tropman and

Morningstar, for instance, investigated the physiological traits associated with entrepreneurship, such as risk and ambiguity tolerance, self-confidence, flexibility, persistence, independence, and so on.[9] Hisrich found that entrepreneurs are on average first-born children, male, college educated, in their thirties when they have their first successful enterprise, energetic, creative, and risk takers.[10] Kuratko and colleagues identified four factors that motivate entrepreneurs: extrinsic rewards, independence/autonomy, intrinsic rewards, and family security.[11]

Another group has investigated the socioeconomic conditions— the "regime"—conducive to the development of entrepreneurship. Kent, for instance, edited a volume with contributions on the appropriate legal framework, government regulation, and fiscal conditions for entrepreneurship.[12] Tropman and Morningstar identify institutions that are conducive to entrepreneurship.[13] Scase and Goffee discuss the social conditions conducive to entrepreneurship in Europe.[14]

A third group has focused on the contribution of entrepreneurship to economic development. Kilby, for instance, edited a volume with contributions on the role of entrepreneuship in economic development.[15] Capaldo provides evidence of the contribution of entrepreneurship to the economic development of Southern Italy.[16] And Odagiri analyzes the importance of entrepreneurship in the development of Japan's iron and steel industries since the mid-nineteenth century.[17]

A fourth group has focused on entrepreneurship as a source of sustainable competitive advantages. Peter Drucker, for instance, connects entrepreneurship to innovation and competitiveness. Constantine Markides emphasizes the importance of "strategic innovation" (i.e., the turning of market niches to mass markets). Michael Porter emphasizes the importance of "entrepreneurial edge" in the choice of different activities to deliver a unique mix of value.

A fifth group of business strategists emphasizes the importance of relationships among individuals and institutions that enable the entrepreneur to solve complex problems. In this sense, entrepreneurship is a dynamic process:

It necessarily requires links to relationships not only among and between individuals but also among and between a variety of institutions. The stronger, more complex and more diverse the web relationships, the more the entrepreneur is likely to have access to opportunities, the greater the chance of solving problems expeditiously, and ultimately the greater the chance of solving problems expeditiously, and ultimately the greater the success for a new venture.[18]

This view on entrepreneurship is consistent with the approach we have taken throughout this book that the discovery and exploitation of new business opportunities is a matter of integration of market and technical information, which in turn is a matter of both communication and relationships. In preindustrial and early industrial capitalism, the integration of market and technical information was performed by individual proprietors or partners. In late industrial capitalism the integration of market and technical information was performed by professional managers, while in today's post-industrial or network capitalism the integration of market and technical information is performed collectively by entrepreneurial networks. In this sense, entrepreneurship is a dynamic rather than a static concept that has been changing along with capitalism. It has evolved from individual entrepreneurship in preindustrial capitalism to collective entrepreneurship in today's capitalism.

FROM INDIVIDUAL TO COLLECTIVE ENTREPRENEURSHIP

From the merchant era to today, capitalism has undergone three distinct stages: preindustrial and early industrial capitalism (individual capitalism), late industrial capitalism (corporate capitalism), and post-industrial capitalism (network capitalism). Each stage of capitalism features distinct business institutions that allowed capitalism to endure and to adapt to changes to its social environment brought about by new technology, demographic trends, and changes in the ideological and political map of the world economy.

Individual capitalism features small-scale industries consisting of a large number of small-scale enterprises with distinct external boundaries that separate each enterprise from its competitors, suppliers, and customers. Proprietors and partners who perform a dual function as managers and as entrepreneurs normally own small-scale enterprises. As managers, proprietors and partners are involved in the day-to-day business operations, often working side by side with workers and interacting frequently with customers and suppliers. As entrepreneurs, proprietors and partners evaluate and exploit new business opportunities and assume the risks and the rewards associated with them. In this sense, proprietorships and partnerships have no hierarchies, and no internal boundaries to separate ownership from management and managers and workers. Even more, entrepreneurship and management are both performed by the owners of the corporation who stand to assume the enterprise risks and the rewards.

Individual capitalism flourished in the mid-nineteenth century, "when thousands of specialized mercantile establishments operated in the American business system. Most were relatively small, and thus no single firm controlled its field of business. Despite the progress made in industrialization, the output of industrial products remained low enough in volume for merchants to handle directly."[19] The direct involvement of proprietors and partners in the management and the immediate interaction with workers, suppliers, and customers created close internal and external relations that made individual capitalism a personal affair. In this sense, informal family ties and personal trust rather than formal managerial hierarchies ruled internal and external business relations:

For the preindustrial merchant, business was a very personal affair: Merchant firms—especially in Japan, but also in Colonial America (as in the House of Hancock) and Great Britain (as in the House of Baring)—were houses. Relatives were important in the establishment of overseas foreign agencies by British and Colonial American merchants. Personal trust was more important than business organization or managerial hierarchies in the conduct of economic affairs. This was a world of face-to-face contacts.[20]

Small size, day-to-day owner involvement, and face-to-face contacts provide firms in individual capitalism with three major advantages. Day-to-day involvement, for instance, provides owner–managers the technical and market information to deliver low-cost/high-quality products to their customers and to efficiently and effectively adjust their outputs and inputs to changing market conditions. Day-to-day involvement further provides owner–entrepreneurs with the technical and market information for the discovery and exploitation of new business opportunities. The day-to-day interaction of the shoemaker with his customers and suppliers, for instance, enables him to better plan his outputs and inputs and to develop new products such as handbags, leather jackets, and the like. In addition, personal relations and face-to-face contacts create mutual trust and understanding, a sense of community of common fate that minimizes bureaucracy, lower transaction costs, and less chance of shirking and malfeasance.

These advantages of individual capitalism must be weighed against a number of disadvantages, however. Small size, for instance, constrains the ability of firms to attain economies of scale and the cost advantages associated with it. In fact, some industries, such as railroads and iron and steel, are conducive to economies of scale and therefore proprietors and partnerships are inappropriate forms of organization for such industries altogether. A large number of small firms often creates excess competition and market gluts that lead to bankruptcies, which in turn creates market shortages. Proprietorships and partnerships are further unable to assume the high risks associated with expansion to larger and unknown markets. In addition, proprietorships and partnerships often lack the market and technological capabilities and the specialized managerial knowledge to handle larger and more complicated projects. In fact, the technological and financial limitations of individual capitalism were already evident in the mid-nineteenth century in a number of industries. In iron and steel, for instance, "moving the iron from one stage to another was a major problem, for iron makers lacked the resources and market knowledge needed to produce the iron at proper times and ship it to the right places."[21]

Corporate capitalism features large-scale industries consisting of large and complex corporations with distinct external boundaries that separate each one from its suppliers, distributors, customers, and competitors. Hundreds or often thousands of known and unknown stockholders, who normally perform neither the managerial nor the entrepreneurial function, are the owners of large corporations. Stockholders have delegated both functions to professional managers who are normally neither owners nor workers. In this way, internal boundaries are clear-cut lines that separate managers from stockholders and managers from workers.

In this divided corporation, the nominal and the practical authority of allocating corporate resources is vested with managers. As A. A. Berle puts it,

Within the corporation, the management disposes of the aggregate possibility of use, production, and creation in respect of the assets it has collected. Nominally, the corporate management receives this by authority of its stockholders; factually, the process is not a matter of choice on either side.[22]

Indeed, given the large size and the complexity of the majority of corporations, stockholders have no choice but to delegate authority to professional managers. Mansel G. Blackford writes, "As industrial firms grew in size and complexity, the personal management of typical preindustrial times gave way to bureaucratic management. Companies became too large and too complex to be run as one-man shows."[23] In this way, and by contrast to individual capitalism, corporate capitalism is an impersonal system of impersonal formal wage contracts rather than personal formal contracts and supervision. As Thorstein Veblen put it more than six decades ago,

[The corporation] is an incorporation of absentee ownership, wholly and obvious. Hence it is necessarily impersonal in all its contacts and dealings, whether with other business concerns or with workmen employed in the industry. . . . By insensible degrees, as the volume of industry grew larger, employing a larger equipment and larger numbers of workmen, the business concerns necessarily also increased in size and in the volume of transactions, personal supervision of the work by owners was no longer practicable, and personal contact and personal arrangements between the employer–owner and his workmen tapered off into impersonal wage contracts governed by custom and adjusted to the minimum which the traffic would bear.[24]

Impersonal wage contracts eventually turned into formal hierarchies that raised the boundaries that divided stockholders from managers and managers from labor.

In crude summation, most "owners" own stock, insurance savings and pension claims and the like, and do not manage; most managers (corporate administrators) do not own. The corporate collective holds legal title to the tangible productive wealth of the country—for the benefit of others.[25]

Moreover, the introduction of Taylor's system of production led to the creation of multidivisional structures, adding more layers of management between labor and management and more bureaucracy to the organization.

Nevertheless, large size, professional management, and stockholder ownership provide firms in corporate capitalism with a number of advantages. Large size, for instance, allows corporations to mass produce commodities (i.e., attain economies of scale and the cost savings associated with it). This is especially the case for the United States, which gave birth to such corporations. Indeed, Mansel G. Blackford observed

American industrialists achieved high-volume, low-cost production in the processing of liquids, agricultural goods, and metals after the Civil War. This accomplishment of mass production, encouraged by the existence of a large national market and made possible by technological breakthroughs, led to the rise of big business, fundamentally altering the nature of the business firm in the United States.[26]

Large size and the mass production and economies of scale associated with it allowed corporations to weather a price war easier than smaller corporations. Rockefeller's Standard Oil Corporation illustrates this point. Thanks to economies of scale, Standard Oil's kerosene cost fell from 2.5 cents in 1879 to 0.4 cents by 1885, underselling foreign competitors from Europe, Russia, and Southeast Asia.[27] Germany's BASF, Bayer, and Hoechst are additional illustrations of the point. The price of Alizarin, a new yarn dye, fell from 200 marks a kilo in 1878 to 9 marks by 1886, underselling domestic and foreign competitors.[28]

Corporations could quickly expand their size and capacity either through horizontal mergers and acquisitions (i.e., by acquiring and merging with competitors) or through vertical mergers (i.e., by acquiring and merging with their suppliers, distributors, and retailers). In the case of Rockefeller's Standard Oil, in the beginning the company grew by acquiring or driving out of business its competitors. Then it strengthened its position by building its own oil pipelines and by acquiring refiners, distributors, retailers, railway companies, and gas and electric companies. In New York, for instance, Standard Oil Corporation's subsidiary, the Greater New York Public Corporation, had a total of thirty-one subsidiaries of its own: twenty-one oil and gas companies and ten transportation companies. In this way, Standard Oil was turned into a conglomerate that expanded both horizontally, controlling close to 90 percent of the oil market, and vertically, controlling the entire oil supply chain from R&D to extraction, refining, transportation, energy, and marketing.

Professional management allows large corporations to acquire managerial skills, logistics, and technology not often found in individual proprietorships and partnerships.[29] This is especially the case for global corporations that deal with many products and prices at the same time. In fact, the rise of professional management is often quoted as one of the factors that contributed to the success of American corporations during the last quarter of the nineteenth century. American managers like Frederick Taylor and Alfred Sloan brought a revolution in the ways large corporations were organized and managed.[30]

Stockholder ownership allows large corporations to amass enormous amounts of capital and to spread the risks. This is especially the case for the development of products that require large investments in fixed capital and technology. It is also true for companies that are expanding in emerging markets, where conditions can change abruptly. As is the case with professional management, the rise of finance capital is another factor quoted as a source of success of American capitalism in the last quarter of the nineteenth century. Again, innovative American financiers like the Rothschilds, the Belmonts, the Mortons, and the Morgans started their own revolution in the financing of large corporations.[31]

These advantages of corporate capitalism must be weighed against a number of disadvantages. One disadvantage of corporate capitalism is the internal boundaries that separate owners (stockholders) from managers/entrepreneurs. Such boundaries have placed a wedge between the interests of stockholders and managers. Stockholders, for instance, are interested in cutting expenses and raising profits that translate into higher dividends or stock appreciation. By contrast, managers are concerned with power, prestige, and emoluments. This means that strategies that pursue the interests of managers often do not pursue the interests of stockholders. In the case of R.J.R. Nabisco, for years the company produced mediocre results for its stockholders. Yet its management enjoyed a lavish lifestyle, flying from golf course to golf course around the country in corporate jets. The case of Time, Inc. is another case in point. In the late 1980s, the company became the takeover target of Paramount Communications (now part of Viacom Corporation), which offered a hefty premium over the Time, Inc. market price. Yet the management of Time, Inc. rejected the takeover bid, merging instead with Warner Bros. Certainly such a strategy worked for the management of Time, Inc., who kept their posts, but it did not work for the stockholders. Years later, the stock price of Time-Warner was below that offered by Paramount Communications.

The separation of management and control from ownership and the large corporate size have further diminished both their entrepreneurial and their managerial functions, eventually turning them into central planning units rather than true enterprises, microcosms of the planned economy of the former Soviet Union. In this sense

The corporation becomes the legal "owner" of the capital thus collected and has complete decision-making power over it; the corporation runs on its own economic steam. On the other hand, its stockholders, by now grandsons or great grand-sons of the original "investors" or (far more often) transferees of their transferees at thousands of removes, have and expect to have through their stock the "beneficial ownership," of the assets and profits thus accumulated and realized, after taxes, by the corporate enterprise. Management thus becomes, in an odd sort way, the uncontrolled administrator of a kind of trust having the privilege of perpetual accumulation. The stockholder is the passive beneficiary, not only of the original "trust," but of the compounded annual accretions to it.[32]

In this way, stockholder boards by and large become the "passive instrument" of "uncontrolled administrators," and, as is the case in centrally planned economies, large corporations turn into hierarchical organizations. According to J. K. Galbraith,

In the mature corporation, however, the stockholders are without power; the board of directors is normally the passive instrument of the management; decisions, since complexity is usually associated with importance, are effectively the work of groups. These decisions move up through the organization more characteristically than down. It follows that the conventional image of the organization—the customary organization chart is misleading. So accordingly, will be any analysis which uses it as a guide in relating individuals and groups to the corporation.[33]

To put it differently, corporate capitalism is a hybrid of a market system and central planning, especially in its later stage in the 1950s and 1960s, and many large corporations have grown to a size that often exceeds that of single national economies. When one looks at corporate capitalism as a whole, it still remains a market system, and firms are still privately owned and interact with each other through markets. But when one looks at corporate capitalism as separate units, it is a centrally planned system in the sense that all important decisions are taken at the top and direct communication among lower-level members from different divisions is not permitted.

Another disadvantage of corporate capitalism is the internal boundaries that separate labor from management, especially the multilayers of middle management that block the flow of information between workers who get the job done and top management who does the planning in the corporate headquarters. As discussed in previous chapters, such internal boundaries are an impediment to the efficient and effective functioning of the corporation, especially in a rapidly changing environment like that of a global economy.

At this point, one must ask an important question, however. If large corporations have been bureaucratic and inefficient, how could they be so successful in introducing a host of innovations that transformed the world economy? The answer to this question is twofold. First, to some extent the advantages of the economies of scale and the amassing of large sums of capital for the development of large and complex products outweigh the disadvantages. This is particularly the case for capital- and technology-intensive industries such as automobiles, railroads, and shipbuilding. Second, as discussed earlier, the rise of large corporations was inevitably associated with market control and the restriction of competition that turned firms from competing against each other to competing against consumers:

Decisions previously made through the free interplay of market forces came to be internalized within the new gigantic firms. The invisible hand of the market gave way to the visible hand of business management in ordering and coordinating the American economy. In some key industries, oligopoly developed and competition lessened as big businesses grew in importance.[34]

In the 1880s, for instance, most of the major U.S. industries were dominated by trusts and pools that restricted market entry and competition. As Heilbroner and Singer put it, "By the 1880s there was a cordage pool, a whiskey pool, a coal pool, a salt pool, and endless rail and other pools. For the growing scale of individual firms provided a strong new impulse to avoid the mutual bloodletting of cutthroat competition."[35]

In addition, as discussed in Chapter 2, the rise of large corporations coincided with multinationalization, a period when the world economy was a collection of separate national and local markets rather than a single integrated global market. In such a regime, large corporations established local and national sanctuaries that sealed them from competition. As a result, they could survive and prosper in spite of their internal inefficiencies. As globalization resumed its course in the last twenty years, the disadvantages of corporate capitalism began to outweigh its advantages and corporate capitalism also had its place in history. It was succeeded by network capitalism.

Network capitalism features a new breed of market institutions that combine the flexibility and personal touch of individual capitalism with the economies of scale, professional management, and financing capabilities of large corporations of corporate capitalism. Specifically, network capitalism consists of entrepreneurial networks that, like spider webs, spread over large and small corporations, turning them into collective entrepreneurships; that is, institutions that provide for the communication, the incentives, and the relationships that let their members share the risks and rewards of information sharing and information integration for the discovery and exploitation of new business opportunities. In this sense, collective entrepreneurship reunites the functions of management and entrepreneurship and places them in the hands of the true owners as they existed in proprietorships and partnerships of individual capitalism. This means that the members of collective entrepreneurships can communicate directly with each other and quickly integrate market and technical information for the discovery and exploitation of new business opportunities. As Dent puts it,

Networks don't have a sluggish bureaucracy. A premium is placed on delivering information at light speed, when and where is needed, not in slowing everything down in heaps of red tape, petty power plays, and emotional problems. The new network model is a radical change in business structure and practice that changes the role of every person within the organization.[36]

In practice, entrepreneurial networks are strategic alliances of inventors, innovators, manufacturers, distributors, retailers, and customers sharing the risks and rewards of their partnership. Strategic alliances describe the formation of entrepreneurial webs or networks among several corporations that allow them to pursue multiproduct development and distribution that they could not have pursued otherwise. Entrepreneurial networks combine both large organization size and small production batches catered to different market segments. In this sense, entrepreneurial networks combine both economies of scale and economies of scope, a hybrid strategy often called "mass customization."

The formation of entrepreneurial networks both within and across corporations is particularly important for the development of complex products that require extensive technical knowledge scattered both inside and outside corporate boundaries, in marketing departments, distribution centers, private and public databases, and private and public research departments. Automobile companies, for instance, form technical alliances with several parts and components suppliers to design, develop, and manufacture new automobiles.[37] Computer and telecommunications companies form alliances to develop new products such as cellular phones and network equipment, and Internet retailers form alliances with distributors and marketers. Corporate alliances also allow corporations to share the risks of entering new markets, especially emerging markets. Alliances are also present in the airline industry, where airlines team up to jointly market their services and to better utilize their routes.

Reflecting this trend, the number of corporate alliances in the information-technology industry rose from 196 in 1984 to 4,358 in 1994. Alliances are particularly present in industries most affected by globalization, such as the computer, telecommunications, and consumer electronics industries. Throughout the same period, AT&T formed 127 alliances, IBM 74, Ericson 62, and Siemens 61.[38] Alliances are also present in industries such as food and beverage and pharmaceuticals that have been expanding rapidly in emerging markets where market information is limited and of poor quality. In 1994, for instance, foreign companies formed 294 alliances in the Soviet Union, 270 in the People's Republic of China, 247 in Hong Kong, 239 in South Korea, and 179 in Taiwan.[39] Alliances are also formed between companies of mature countries wishing to enter the markets of other mature countries. American and European companies form alliances to enter the Japanese market while Japanese and U.S. companies form alliances to enter the European markets.

In short, each capitalist stage featured distinct business institutions that are summarized in Exhibit 5.1. Individual capitalism is personal capitalism with the individual owner–manager entrepreneur at the center of economic action. Individual industries consist of independent small-scale enterprises owned by individual proprietors and partners who perform both a managerial and an entrepreneurial function, and at times work side by side with labor. In this sense, individual capitalism is a system with well-defined market institutions. Firms have no internal boundaries to separate owner–entrepreneurs from managers and managers from workers. But firms do have external boundaries that separate them from their competitors, suppliers, distributors, and customers.

Managerial capitalism is impersonal capitalism with professional managers at the center of economic action. Individual industries consist of a small number of large-scale enterprises owned by stockholders and managed by professional managers who rarely perform any direct labor. In this sense, corporate capitalism is also a system with well-defined institutions. Large corporations have well-defined external and internal boundaries. External boundaries separate each corporation from its suppliers, distributors, and customers. Internal

Exhibit 5.1
From Individual to Network Capitalism: The Rising and Falling of
Internal and External Corporate Boundaries

	Firm Size	External Boundaries	Internal Boundaries	Ownership/Management Entrepreneurship
Individual Capitalism	Small	Distinct	Nonexistent	Unified
Managerial Capitalism	Large	Distinct	Distinct	Separated
Network Capitalism	Large	Blurred	Blurred	Unified

boundaries separate stockholder–owners from manager–nonowners and workers.

Network capitalism is a hybrid of personal and impersonal capitalism, with collective entrepreneurship at the center of the action. Individual industries consist of entrepreneurial networks owned and managed by their members. In this sense, network capitalism is a system without well-defined institutions (i.e., they do not have well-defined external boundaries). Entrepreneurial networks are alliances of suppliers, producers, distributors, and customers, often alliances among former competitors rather than distinct corporations in the conventional sense of the term, an issue to be further addressed in the following section.

TYPES OF COLLECTIVE ENTREPRENEURSHIP

As discussed, collective entrepreneurship is about structures that afford the opportunity and the incentive to individuals both inside and outside conventional corporations as well as individuals across corporations to share and integrate technical and market information for the discovery and the exploitation of new business. This does not mean that entrepreneurial networks hold referendums to decide which new products to develop or which new markets to pursue, but it has created structures that afford the opportunity to the hundreds or even thousands of hidden entrepreneurs scattered among suppliers, distributors, customers, and collaborators to come forward with the information they possess and to join forces for the discovery and the exploitation of new business opportunities. Collective entrepreneurship can be further developed within well-defined explicit formal relations or within not-well-defined informal implicit relations.

Collective entrepreneurship can be classified in two parallel ways: internal versus external and contractual versus noncontractual.

Internal Collective Entrepreneurship

Internal entrepreneurship is developed inside conventional corporations as a result of the lowering of internal boundaries that separate stockholders from management and managers from workers (see Exhibit 5.2). In this way, stockholders can share market and technical information and work together with management and labor for the development and exploitation of new business opportunities.

As discussed briefly in Chapter 4, the lowering of internal boundaries is not just a matter of hardware technology, such as the building of internal information highways, intranets, groupware, or voice mail, but is also a matter of institutions, such as job rotation and transfers, teamwork, bonuses, and stock options. Job rotation, labor transfers, and teamwork, for instance, allow the members of the corporation to develop contextual knowledge (i.e., knowledge about the entire pro-

Exhibit 5.2
Internal Collective Entrepreneurship: Lowering the Internal Boundaries of Conventional Corporations

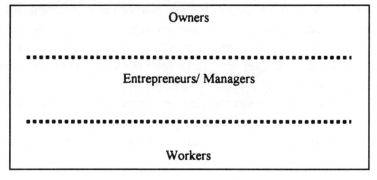

duction process rather than about pieces of it). Bonuses and stock options allow organization members to share the risks and rewards associated with the discovery and exploitation of new business opportunities that often replace older business that either competition or new technology has turned obsolete.

External Collective Entrepreneurship

External collective entrepreneurship is developed across the external boundaries of conventional corporations in two ways, vertically and horizontally (see Exhibit 5.3). External vertical entrepreneurship is developed forward, between manufacturers, distributors, and customers, and backward, with suppliers. It takes the form of a genuine alliance among independent companies or the alliance of the former pieces of a large conglomerate. A good example of external vertical collective entrepreneurship is that developed among petroleum corporations and utility corporations as a source of fuels (upstream), and with energy companies for the marketing of bundled energy products (downstream).[40] Another example is that developed between computer manufacturers such as Dell and it suppliers, distributors, and customers. A third example is that of former conglomerates, like AT&T and ITT, that divided themselves into independent companies. AT&T, for instance, spun off its equipment maker Lucent Technologies to its stockholders, turning a parent–subsidiary relation into an alliance.

Petroleum, computer, and telecommunications companies are not the only ones forming vertical corporate alliances. Retailers, such as Costco, Dillard, Home Depot, Kmart, and Walmart routinely cooperate with manufacturers on product packaging and shipping and on inventory issues. Some manufacturers like Black and Decker will even cooperate with retailers like Home Depot for the development of new products.

External horizontal collective entrepreneurship is developed across corporations making complimentary products or similar products, such as technology products. Collective entrepreneurship can range from equity positions to joint product and marketing agreements,

Exhibit 5.3
External Collective Entrepreneurship

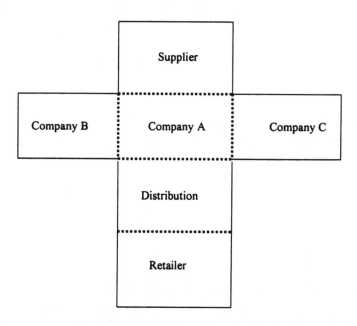

joint transportation and distribution agreements to franchise agreements. A good example of horizontal collective entrepreneurship is that between two former competitors, IBM and Storage Tek, for the development and marketing of high-end storage devices. Specifically, Storage Tek agreed to confine itself to the production of the storage devices and IBM to market them under its own label. The two companies also agreed to cooperate with each other for the development of the next generation of diskdrives.[41] Another good example of collective entrepreneurship is that between Dr. Pepper and Seven-Up for the joint promotion of their brands. Specifically, the two companies agreed to raise their marketing spending by 25 percent in 1998 with advertising promotions in ESPN and MTV, targeting the eighteen to twenty-four age group.[42] A third example of collective entrepreneurship is that between AT&T Network systems and Hewlett-Packard for the development of a communications network for home shopping, interactive games, and video on demand. A fourth example is that between Sony Corporation and Sanyo Corporation for the development of large flat-panel displays.[43] A fifth example is that of IBM and its competitor, Toshiba. The two companies have been working closely together for the joint development of semiconductors.

In short, collective entrepreneurship can be formed in two ways: internally, by lowering the internal boundaries of the conventional corporation, and externally, by lowering the external boundaries of the conventional corporation. Depending on the purpose, duration, type, and conditions of agreements among network members, collective entrepreneurship can be further distinguished between contractual and noncontractual (see Exhibit 5.4).

Contractual Collective Entrepreneurship

Contractual entrepreneurial networks are short-term, formal, and explicit agreements regarding the purpose of their formation, their duration, and the contribution of resources of each member and the allocation of the expected rewards. Contractual networks are open networks; that is, they may expand or contract according to market opportunities and, therefore, can flourish in environments of high mobility of highly skilled people, like mid-career professionals, hardware and software engineers, production control managers, and marketing experts (see Exhibit 5.4). They also work better in production processes with a low degree of interdependence and integration. In the filmmaking industry, for instance, contractual networks are formed by writers, producers, actors, and so on for specific projects and dissolved after the project has been completed. In such industries, "uncertainty and demand volatility require film-makers to develop competencies in: the identification and recruitment of talented commercial and artistic project participants; and the management of complexities spanning coordination of cast, production crews, elaborate sets and sophisticated audio, visual and special effects technologies."[44] In the book publishing industry, entrepreneurial networks are formed among authors, editors, publishers, distributors, and retailers. They explicitly specify the function of each party and the form of compensation.

Exhibit 5.4
Contractual versus Noncontractual Entrepreneurial Networks

	Contractual	Noncontractual
Purpose	Specific	Vague
Duration	Short term	Long term
Agreement	Explicit	Implicit
Conditions	High mid-career mobility; low degree of interdependence	Low mid-career mobility; high degree of interdependence
Objective	Cost cutting	Product/ technology

Due to their openness, contractual networks can draw members from several companies, research institutes, and universities and be revolutionary (i.e., develop breakthrough ideas and products that create entirely new industries), and therefore are more appropriate for industries that rely on creativity, such as software development, entertainment, and publishing, rather than those industries that require conformity and attention to detail, such as automobiles and consumer electronics. In addition, because of their short-term nature, contractual networks are suitable for industries with a high degree of component standardization. They are also suitable for declining industries, and for industries that are concerned with short-term cost reductions.[45]

In the high-technology industries, contractual networks, known as "teams of expert integrators," have contributed to the catching up of American companies with their Japanese counterparts in global industries. Though modeled after those of Japan, U.S. corporate alliances, research consortia, and expert teams display their own peculiarities and specificity, reflecting a number of local conditions, such as formal and explicit contracts, individualism, and high interfirm mobility. Such conditions lead to the creation of open formal contractual networks for specific products and processes rather than informal and vague networks, as is the case with the Overseas Ethnic Chinese Group (OECG) and Japanese *keiretsu* groups. Indeed, Marco Iansiti and Jonothan West confirm that a number of American companies have, indeed, in their own way, fended off the Japanese challenge through the formation of corporate alliances, research consortia, and teams of experts.[46] Major software makers such as Microsoft, IBM, and Oracle have formed hundreds of alliances for the development, marketing, and distribution of new products.

Contractual networks may be limited to private parties or may extend to government entities. In the United States, for instance, entrepreneurial networks are primarily limited to private companies, with the exception of nonprofit research institutions, such as universities and government agencies, that collaborate with private companies. The alliance between the Environmental Defense Fund, a national environmental concern on the one side, and McDonald's and General Motors on the other, is a case in point.[47] In Europe, entrepreneurial networks are often mixed; they include private corporations and government agencies, especially semiprivatized government monopolies. A good example of such a network is the European Strategic Programme for Research and Development in Information Technology (ESPRIT), formed in the early 1980s among Bull, Siemens, Compagnie Generale, Philips, Plessy, Thomson, Olivieti, and the European Community (now European Union).

Irrespective of the direction of the extension, contractual networks are subject to two limitations that eventually constrain their members from internalizing the rewards of their partnership. First, key network members may pull out of the network as soon as their contractual obligation expires and form new networks that may become formidable competitors with the old network. Two good examples of such possibilities are Bill Gates, who quit IBM to form Microsoft, and Steve Jobs, who quit Apple Computer to form Next Inc. Second, the possibility of key members quitting contractual networks and the short lifespan of such networks make it difficult for members to exploit the benefits associated with experience learning.

Noncontractual Networks

Noncontractual entrepreneurial networks are networks based on long-term informal, implicit, and vague agreements regarding the purpose of their formation, the duration, and the contribution and rewards of each member (see Exhibit 5.4). Noncontractual networks are closed networks; that is, they are limited to long-term partners. In this sense, noncontractual networks are conducive to long-term investments in partnership assets that create a high degree of mutual interdependence among partners. Such mutual interdependence allows members to internalize the benefits of any discoveries better and to fully exploit the economies associated with what is known as the "experience curve." Specifically, mutual interdependence allows noncontractual networks to share information and coordinate interdependent tasks, invest in project-specific tasks, and rely on trust rather than formal contracts, a factor that lowers transaction costs.[48] In this sense, noncontractual networks are suitable for industries that produce complex products that require interfirm coordination. In addition, they work better in expanding industries where corporations are eventually faced with resource shortages, and for the pursuit of long-term objectives such as the development of basic technologies and megaprojects that take a long time to complete.[49]

Two good examples of noncontractual networks are those of OECG in Southeast Asia and *keiretsu* groups in Japan. OECG entrepreneurial networks are formed among extended family members with close contacts to government agencies, especially to state-controlled financial institutions.[50] As family organizations, OECGs rely heavily on *guanxi*, an implicit code of mutual reciprocity and fair treatment for the discovery and the exploitation of new business opportunities. Network members who fail to reciprocate or be fair are ostracized (i.e., expelled from the network and subjected to a smear campaign that makes it next to impossible for them to join another network). In this sense, reputation and loss of prestige function as safeguards against opportunism, a behavior pattern that could threaten the integrity and cohesiveness of the network.

Dividing the world into *guanxi* and non-*guanxi* members or to insiders versus outsiders allows business activities to be performed through channels not accessible to outsiders. In this sense, *guanxi* provides an advantage to companies that rely on personal marketing like the selling of financial products. In fact, a number of studies of foreign companies in China confirm that *guanxi* can have a positive impact on a company's bottom line, especially for companies that have developed *guanxi* relations for a long time.[51]

Though they are large organizations, the coordination structure of OECGs is based more on informal *guanxi* relations cultivated over time by their founders and less on formal contractual relationships. Specifically, the coordination structure of a typical OECG consists of a core leadership that oversees a number of holding companies, which in turn oversee a number of subsidiaries. The core leadership normally is assumed by the founding kin or the founding clan members who appoint the leadership of the holding companies and the holding company subsidiaries. In this sense, OECGs have no internal boundaries to separate owners from management, and that allows their members to communicate efficiently and effectively and is an incentive for hard work. As Weidenbaum has put it,

The combination of owners and managers avoids many of the "agency" problems that Western businesses face in getting executives to promote the interests of shareholders. Within this framework, the Chinese family firm provides a high degree of flexibility accompanied by intense managerial effort. These desirable traits are encouraged by ties of mutual obligation.[52]

In short, an OECG is an informal business network organization that relies more on personal connections, mutual obligations, trust, and reputation as safeguards against opportunistic behavior than on hierarchies. OECGs are crossborder and allow their members to reap certain sustainable competitive advantages over outsiders, advantages that can be found in a similar network organization, the Japanese corporate alliances and *keiretsu* groups.

As is the case with OECGs, Japanese corporate alliances and *keiretsu* groups are founded on interpersonal relations, mutual trust, and reciprocal obligations among their members, as well as the prestige and reputation of each member, rather than hierarchies and contractual obligations, with one difference. Kinship and clanship is not as important as in the OECGs. *Keiretsu* groups are bound together by cross-stock ownership and business deals. It is estimated that in 1989 about 40 percent of all publicly held stock in Japan was locked in cross-ownership holdings among corporations. Specifically, 26.51 percent of Sumitomo stock was owned by Sumitomo firms; 25.5 percent of Mitsui stock was owned by Mitsui companies; and 24.6 percent of Mitsubishi stock was owned by Mitsubishi firms. Toyota, for instance, controls 23.1 percent of Toyota Automatic Loom works, 21.2 percent of Aichi Steel Works, 48.3 percent of Kanto Autoworks, and so on.[53]

Depending upon objectives and structure, *keiretsu* can be classified into three categories: banking, enterprise, and supplier–buyer. A banking *keiretsu* is a group of companies organized around a "main" bank and tied together through cross-stockholding relations. Group members share the same source of financing, utilize the same channels of marketing, and distribute trade with insiders. An enterprise *keiretsu* is a business group clustered around a large company producing complex products, supporting its main operations, and contributing by its efforts to develop new products. A supplier–buyer *keiretsu* is a business group that consists of core companies producing complex products made from a large number of parts produced by peripheral companies on a subcontracting basis.

Keiretsu relations are rationalized in different ways. Banking *keiretsu*, for instance, allow their members to enjoy low-cost financing and to attain certain economies of scale associated with information sharing and the utilization of common distribution and marketing channels. Enterprise *keiretsu* allows the business groups to combine the economies of scale associated with a large organization and the diversification and economies of scope associated with separate enterprises. Supplier–buyer *keiretsu* allow buyer companies to exert some control over subcontractors, but without limiting the autonomy and flexibility that often become a source of creativity. In this sense, a supplier–buyer *keiretsu* allows a business group to develop certain "core competencies" which can only be achieved through a large organization of small individualized production batches, competencies that are crucial in complex products, like automobiles, machine tools, and consumer electronics, which Japanese companies have sustained an advantage in over a long period of time. At least, this is the finding of an empirical study of the Japanese and American automobile industries.[54]

In short, as was the case with OECGs, *keiretsu* groups are network organizations founded on informal relations between members that share common interests. Being informal, *keiretsu* groups combine the advantages of both markets and hierarchies. Their organizations are large and their production scales are small, allowing them to attain economies of scale.

As was the case with contractual entrepreneurial networks, noncontractual entrepreneurial networks can be formed among private parties or among private parties and government agencies. A good example of a semiprivate noncontractual network is the very large scale integrated circuits (VLSI) Technology Research Association founded in the late 1970s between the Japanese government (MITI) and semiconductor manufacturers (NEC, Toshiba, Hitachi, Fujitsu, and Mitsubishi) for the development of a new generation of computer chips. Another example is that formed between Chinese state-owned corporations and OECG. A third example is that formed between the Korean government and the *chaebols*, large Korean conglomerates, for the development of important technologies, such as semiconductors and consumer electronics.

Yet noncontractual networks have their own limitations: Limited to long-term partners, they are evolutionary rather than revolutionary; that is, they are conducive to marginal rather than radical innovations. In this sense, noncontractual networks are more appropriate for industries that require a longer product development cycle and emphasis on detail, like consumer electronics, machine tools, and automobiles.

Successful contractual entrepreneurship may be eventually converted into noncontractual entrepreneurship. Conversely, noncontractual entrepreneurship may be converted to contractual entrepreneurship.[55] Experimenting with alliances of different length, Doz found that alliances are evolutionary, in that they normally proceed from short-term project-specific alliances (contractual in our terminology) to long-term multiproject alliances.[56]

In short, in capitalism, firms perform a dual function as managerial and as entrepreneurial units. In preindustrial and industrial capitalism, firm owners, proprietors, and partners perform both functions. In corporate capitalism, owners and stockholders delegate both functions to professional management. In network capitalism, entrepreneurial networks perform both functions. In this sense, entrepreneurial networks are more like communities of common fate and less like conventional corporations, an issue to be addressed in the next chapter.

NOTES

1. Barreto, 1989, p. 48.
2. Adam Smith, for instance, identified entrepreneurship with both management and organization of businesses. Alfred Marshal also identified entrepreneurship with management.
3. Baumol, 1993, p. 200.
4. Casson, 1982, p. 9.
5. Joseph A. Schumpeter, *Capitalism, Socialism, and Democracy* (New York: Harper and Brothers, 1950), p. 132.
6. Kirzner, 1984, p. 42.
7. Ibid., p. 50.
8. Hammer and Champy, 1993, p. 26.
9. Tropman and Morningstar, 1989, p. 3.

10. Hisrich, 1986.

11. Kuratko, Hornsby, and Neffziger, 1997.

12. Kent, 1984.

13. Tropman and Morningstar, 1989.

14. Scase and Goffee, 1987.

15. Kilby, 1971.

16. Capaldo, 1997.

17. Y. Odagiri, "The Development of Japan's Iron and Steel Industries," in *The Entrepreneuer in Economic Theory*, ed. M. Casson (Totowa, NJ: Barnes and Noble Books, 1982).

18. Smilor, 1986, p. 52.

19. Blackford and Kerr, 1986, p. 107.

20. Blackford, 1988, p. 27.

21. Ibid., p. 110.

22. Berle, 1954, p. 31.

23. Ibid., pp. 55–56.

24. Veblen, 1923, pp. 83, 105.

25. Berle and Means, 1968, p. x.

26. Ibid., pp. 51–52.

27. Chandler, 1990, p. 130.

28. Ibid.

29. At least, that is traditionally the case for large American corporations.

30. Chandler, 1990.

31. Josephson, 1962.

32. Ibid., p. xv.

33. Galbraith, 1978, p. 156.

34. Blackford and Kerr, 1986, p. 153.

35. Heilbroner and Singer, 1984, p. 197.

36. Dent, 1998, p. 136.

37. The alliances between Mazda and Ford and between GM and Isuzu are two examples.

38. Nicholas S. Vonortas and Stratos J. Safioleas, "Strategic Alliances in Information Technology and Developing Country Firms: Recent Evidence," *World Development*, 25 (5): 1997, pp. 659–661.

39. Ibid., p. 663.

40. Crump, 1997.

41. Weber, 1996, p. B4.

42. Benerza, 1997, p. 1.

43. Tsuchiyama, 1996.

44. DeFillippi and Arthur, 1998, p. 125.

45. Dyer, Dong, and Chu, 1998, p. 72.

46. M. Iansiti and J. West, "Technology Integration: Turning Great Research into Great Products," *Harvard Business Review*, May-June 1997.

47. Hemphill, 1996.

48. For details, see Dyer, Dong, and Chu, 1998, p. 58.

49. Ibid., p. 72.

50. Arayama and Mourdoukoutas, 1999a.

51. For survey results and literature review, see Yadong Luo, 1997, and T.K.P. Leng, Y. H. Wong, and Syson Wong, 1997.

52. Weidenbaum, 1996, pp. 142–143.

53. For details, see Mourdoukoutas, 1993, Exhibits 3.6 and 3.7.

54. Dyer, Dong, and Chu, 1998.

55. For a detailed discussion of entrepreneurial relations in marketing, see Vlosky and Wilson, 1997.

56. Doz, 1996.

Chapter 6

Communities of Common Fate

> As companies focus on their core activities and outsource the rest, their success increasingly depends on their ability to control what happens in the value chain outside their own boundaries.
>
> —Victor Fung[1]

> A society which fails to fully provide for the creation of multi-firm industry collaboration will inefficiently produce leaky property and, in a world market, will suffer in competition with a society which is more completely equipped with a range of institutional forms.
>
> —William G. Ouchi and Michele Kremen Bolton

History has many surprises for true believers. For decades, Marxists and their disciples dreamed of a capitalist alternative, a system that put workers in charge of their work and the outcome of their work. Today, at the threshold of the new millennia, Marxists' dreams seem to have come true, not within a socialist system, but within a variant of conventional capitalism, network capitalism.

As discussed in previous chapters, in network capitalism, conventional hierarchical corporations are gradually transformed into entrepreneurial networks that allow their members to share the risks and rewards from the discovery and exploitation of new business opportunities. Entrepreneurial networks have no internal boundaries separating stockholders from managers and managers from workers. Neither do they have external boundaries separating them from suppliers, distributors, retailers, customers, and even competitors. In this sense, entrepreneurial networks look more like communities of common fate bound together by a common vision (i.e., by a mission and core values rather than by contractual relations). As Charlan Jeanne Nemeth has put it, "Most companies, even those considered 'visionary,' emphasize mechanisms of social control rather than innovation. They recognize the power of clear goals, worker participation, consistent feedback, a cohesive work force, and a reward system that underscores desired behaviors and values."[2]

If entrepreneurial networks look more like communities of common fate and less like conventional corporations, certain business principles and strategies that are effective for conventional corporations are not effective for entrepreneurial networks. Take Hammer and Champy's business strategy of the division of labor by process (reengineering), for instance, which we discussed in Chapter 3. Not only has reengineering approached its limits as a source of sustainable competitive advantage in the 1990s, but it is also of little relevance to understanding how entrepreneurial networks operate and formulate their competitive strategy altogether, for two reasons. First, as in Taylor's division of labor, the business strategy it sought to replace, the focus of reengineering is on labor as the human resource to be allocated to different processes by management. And although the founders of reengineering argue to the opposite, such a focus makes sense for conventional hierarchical corporations where the objective of management is labor control and conformity. But a focus on labor control and conformity does not make sense in entrepreneurial networks where the objective of management is innovation and creativity and the handling of the friction associated with it (see Chapter 4). Besides, since entrepreneurial networks are about relations among independent entrepreneurs rather than relations between labor and management, the focus of business strategy should be on the division of entrepreneurship, not on the division of labor (see Exhibit 6.1). Second, reengineering focuses on one operation, one part of the economic activity, the production of goods and services. In this sense, it is a too narrow business strategy for entrepreneurial networks that extend throughout the product supply chain (i.e., to several operations, resource supply, product development, production/assembly, transportation, distribution, and retailing).

In short, the key to a successful business strategy of entrepreneurial networks is not how skillfully they divide labor by task or by process in the production of goods and services, but rather how skillfully they divide roles in the collection of activities they perform. The skillful allocation of roles among the members of entrepreneurial networks, in turn, is both a matter of logistics and a matter of vision of the network (i.e., a mission and a set of core values that define the rules of conduct in their internal and external relations).

Addressing the new concepts of the community of common fate and the division of entrepreneurship and their importance for business strategy in more detail, the remainder of this chapter is in two sections. The first section is a discussion of the transformation from the conventional corporation to the entrepreneurial community of common fate and the second section is a discussion of the division of entrepreneurship among network members.

FROM THE CONVENTIONAL CORPORATION TO THE ENTREPRENEURIAL COMMUNITY OF COMMON FATE

Pioneered by utopian socialists in the earlier days of industrialization and reintroduced by Robert Cole in the 1970s, "community of fate" is about the common feelings shared among employees of an organization. It is the belief that their economic destinies are interwoven and closely connected to the destiny of their organization. "Community of fate ideology refers to the feeling among employees that all employees of an organization share a similar future, that everyone in the organization will succeed or fail together."[3] As is the

Exhibit 6.1
Division of Entrepreneurship versus Division of Labor

	Division of Labor	Division of Entrepreneurship
Suitable for	Conventional Hierarchical Corporations	Entrepreneurial Networks
Focus on	Labor Control and Conformity	Innovation and Creativity
	Production	Product Supply Chain

case in conventional communities, an entrepreneurial community of common fate is founded more on informal rules, values, and beliefs and less on formal rules and procedures.

When applied to corporations, "community of common fate" is about entrepreneurial networks, corporate alliances, and partnerships sharing a number of common objectives and values. Northwest Airlines, for instance, shares with its partners Alaska Air and KLM Royal Dutch Airlines a similar culture, work ethic, integrity attitude, and reputation. AT&T shares with its partners AT&T Universal Card and Total System a similar work ethic, integrity attitude, company reputation, and skilled labor force. United Parcel Services shares with its partners Lands End and NetDox a similar corporate culture and work ethic as well as a similar corporate reputation.

In this sense, a community of common fate is an advanced stage of collective entrepreneurship, a stage where common goals, common values and beliefs, and informal rules of conduct substitute for hierarchies and formal rules as a means of communication, motivation, and control:

On the most practical level, redefining organizations as communities means using the approaches of community development in organizations, particularly in business organizations. It also means seeing organizations as centers of meaning and larger purpose to which people can commit themselves as free citizens in democratic society.[4]

In this sense, the members of an organization are after something more than material compensation, they are after professional fulfillment and satisfaction, and personal happiness that is closely related to higher productivity and profitability.

Though it is hard to substantiate this proposition empirically, a number of studies support the importance of a community of common fate and the corporate vision that is at the heart of it as a source of sustainable advantage. A sound vision creates a mutual trust among the stakeholders of the corporation and a reputation with customers and suppliers, which are nontransferable assets translating to a sound corporate performance. A *Business Week* survey of 1 thousand corporations confirmed that a clear mission has a positive impact on the company's profit. Indeed, the survey found that corporations with clear mission statements had an average rate of stockholder return of 16.1 percent, while those without a mission statement had a 7.9 percent average rate of return.[5] A Gallup Organization survey of 55 thousand workers found a close correlation between worker happiness and corporate performance.[6] In this sense, a sound vision can be a source of sustainable competitive advantage. As Fung puts it, "Someone might steal our database, but when they call up a supplier, they don't have the long relationship with the supplier that Li & Fung has. It makes a difference to suppliers when they know that you are dedicated to the business, that you've been honoring your commitments for 90 years."[7]

In general, community of common faith can be implemented in the following ways. First is the sharing of the risks and rewards from the discovery and exploitation of new business opportunities. As briefly discussed in Chapter 4, the sharing of risks and rewards from collective entrepreneurship can be implemented through a number of policies that tie member compensation to the performance of the organization, such as bonuses, Employee Stock Ownership Plans, and stock options. Corporate bonuses, for instance, connect the quarterly, semiannual, or yearly compensation of network members to their performance. ESOPs connect the retirement plans of network members to the equity performance of the network. Stock options supplement the compensation of network members with the right to buy the network stock at a given market price. Microsoft's stock option plan is a case in point. Since 1988, the company has issued 807 million stock options to its labor force of a market value of $80 billion; several thousands of Microsoft's 28 thousand employees are stock option millionaires.[8]

Second is the sharing of a common vision (i.e., a common mission and common core values). At the heart of the community of common fate, corporate vision provides for the ideology to win the enthusiastic support of the members of the organization for the introduction and development of new technologies. One of the issues addressed by a company's vision is the different cultures and attitudes among its members, especially for corporations that deal with a diverse labor force around the world. In this case, what is acceptable in one culture may not be acceptable in another. Take the difference in attitudes toward teams in the United States and Japan and Korea, for instance. While in Japan weak team members become a challenge for management and coworkers who assist them to catch up with stronger members, in the United States weak members become the targets of management and coworkers and eventually are expelled from the team and the organization.[9]

The difference in prevailing attitudes in U.S. and Japanese companies is not confined to the formation and functioning of teams; it extends to corporate alliances with suppliers. Korean automakers, for instance, "provide assistance to their suppliers in the areas of quality, cost reduction, factory layout, and inventory control." In this way, "suppliers make relation-specific investments and coordinate their activities closely with their primary automaker customer."[10] Japanese automakers go even further than that; they assist weaker suppliers to catch up with stronger suppliers. Such a practice protects companies from unexpected part shortages, promoting innovation and product development at the same time: "Providing assistance to suppliers is a highly effective method for both helping and forcing suppliers to continuously innovate and improve to stay ahead of the competitors."[11] In some cases, Japanese and Korean automakers assist their American suppliers to become competitive even if those suppliers sell parts to competing automakers.[12] Japanese automakers also assist their partners when they need it the most, in times of economic stagnation and decline. In 1998, for instance, Toyota proceeded with its Asian expansion plans in spite of the economic turmoil in the region.

Third is the broad and equitable participation of network members in the decision-making process of the organization. Participatory management empowers the members of the organization to run the day-to-day affairs of the organization. Empowerment further accommodates innovation and facilitates communication, and reinforces cooperation: "Empowerment and the delegation it implies have strong positive effects. These considerations reflect trust and make it possible for managers to try things without fear of reprisal. Effective empowerment, then, facilitates communication and cooperation."[13]

Fourth is a strong emphasis on improving working conditions. This condition is of particular importance for entrepreneurial networks that rely on employee creativity. A liberal, university-like environment, for instance, is more conducive to creativity than a conservative, oppressive working environment. The same argument can be made regarding the natural conditions of the working environment. Again, Japanese companies such as Toyota, Nissan, and Mazda emphasize the importance of good working conditions, especially recently, as it has become more difficult for them to recruit new employees. In its new factories, for instance, Toyota has tried to reduce the burden of heavy work, create a dustproof working environment, cut down on noise, and make the workplace safer.[14]

Fifth is a strong emphasis on corporate justice and fairness when it comes to annual reviews and raises, promotion, job assignments and the handling of employees' complaints and disputes, and the building of trust that unlocks new ideas. As W. Chan Kim and Renee Mauborgne put it, "Fair process profoundly influences attitudes and behaviors that are critical to high performance. It builds trust and unlocks ideas."[15] Indeed, the cultivation of trust among the members of an organization helps the organization develop sound human-resource management, which is directly related to R&D activity. In surveying 115 subsidiaries of eighty-nine Fortune 500 companies, Kathryn D. Martell and Stephen J. Caroll, Jr. found that human-resource management practices are strongly correlated with subsidiary R&D activity and overall performance.[16] Justice and fairness should not be limited to monetary rewards, however. They should be extended to nonmonetary rewards, such as the allocation of office and parking spaces, recognition awards, and so on. Fair treatment creates common feelings among the members of the company, feelings that align individual interests with those of the corporation. Corporate vision provides the ideological rationalization for working teams and corporate governance provides the coordination and the incentive structures that make teams operational. The same applies for job rotation. To serve its purpose (i.e., the development of contextual knowledge), members of the organization must enthusiastically support such practice, which can happen efficiently only under the proper coordination and incentive structures.

Another factor that cultivates a community of common fate is what Susan Jackson calls "lifestyle benefits," the provision of a number of activities that turn companies into "hometowns." As Jackson observed, Owens Corning, USA, and Ceriden are just a few examples of companies that have created a number of convenience stores that let employees perform a number of after-hours activities without leaving the office. Other corporations offer child care facilities, housing facilities, and even provide for general education.[17]

In short, when applied to business, a community of common fate is about the feelings of the members of an organization of belonging together and that their individual destiny is connected with the collective destiny, the destiny of the entire organization. The community of common fate can be pursued in various ways: sharing the risks and rewards, sharing a common vision, participatory decision making, good working conditions, and corporate justice.

FROM THE DIVISION OF LABOR TO THE DIVISION OF ENTREPRENEURSHIP

As discussed earlier, for decades, firms knew precisely their internal and external boundaries, especially under the system of corporate capitalism. Managers knew the lines that separated them from stockholders and managers, and workers knew the lines that separated them from managers and stockholders. In this sense, the functions of a firm's stakeholders were clearcut and straightforward: Stockholders owned, managers managed, and workers performed the work. Firms also knew the lines that separated them from their suppliers, distributors, retailers, and customers, and above all from competitors. In fact, in corporate capitalism, research and development, production, distribution, marketing, and retailing were considered disjointed, disintegrated operations, even if they were performed within a conglomerate or parent–subsidiary organization model. Indeed, within the hierarchical model of parent–subsidiary, a separate division that is run like an independent corporation handles each operation. In addition, in corporate capitalism, economic activity normally started from the top down with research and development and proceeded to the other operations, down the chain until it reached the end customer (Exhibit 6.2). In other words, corporations developed new products, distributed them to retailers, and launched marketing campaigns to convince consumers to buy them. As the founder of Sony Corporation, Akio Morita said, "Our plan is to lead the public with new products rather than ask them what kind of products they want. The public does not know what is possible, but we do. So instead of doing a lot of market research, we refine our thinking on a product and its use and try to create a market for it by educating and communicating with the public."[18] In this way, producers developed and manufactured products, distributors distributed them to retailers, and retailers to customers. And although producers, distributors, retailers, and customers often merged to form a conglomerate, they nevertheless performed separate and yet tautological roles: Producers produced, distributors distributed, retailers retailed, and customers consumed (see Exhibit 6.3).

In network capitalism, globalization and technology have modified this model of organization in three ways. First, they have restored consumer sovereignty as it existed in individual capitalism (i.e., economic activity begins from the bottom up, from consumers to producers rather than the other way around, as in Exhibit 6.2). As Fung observes, "For the first time retailers are really creating prod-

Exhibit 6.2
Conventional versus Modern Economic Processes

Conventional Economic Process   Modern Economic Process
(Corporate Capitalism)   (Network Capitalism)

Conventional	Modern
R & D	Consumption
Production	Retailing
Distribution	Distribution
Marketing	Marketing
Retailing	Production
Consumption	R & D

ucts, not just sitting in their offices with salesman after salesman showing them samples: 'Do you want to buy this? Do you want to buy that?' Instead, retailers are participating in the design process."[19] In fact, retailers and everyone on the product-supply chain is under intense pressure from consumers for prompt delivery, especially consumers in the saturated markets of developed countries:

Rich consumers in rich countries want things now, and they want them made precisely in the way they wish. They are not content with mass-production uniformity. They will not always wait for a container ship that takes two weeks to cross the Pacific. This is giving birth to a new kind of manufacturing: a long chain of processes that can go right around the world; a global conveyor belt, as it were.[20]

Not only do consumers in rich countries become more demanding; they are often in partnership with other players in the supply chain. Credit card holders, for instance, receive rebates for every dollar they charge. Telephone subscribers receive free airline traveling miles for every dollar they spend on their telephone bills.

Exhibit 6.3
Division of Roles: Entrepreneurial Networks versus Conventional Corporations

	Supplier	Inventor/ Innovator	Manufacturer/ Assembler	Distributor	Retailer	Customer
Supplier	X					
Inventor/ Innovator		X				
Manufacturer/ Assembler			X	XX		
Distributor			XX	X	XX	
Retailer		XX			X	
Customer		XX				X

Key: *X* indicates tautological roles, as was the case in large corporations in corporate capitalism; *XX* indicates nontautological roles, as is the case in entrepreneurial networks in network capitalism.

Second, globalization and new technology have not only blurred the boundaries among conventional corporations, they have also blurred the boundaries among conventional activities like invention, innovation, manufacturing/assembly, distribution, retailing, and consumption, turning them from independent to interdependent operations (see Exhibit 6.2). Relation-specific investments, for instance, like those between automakers, have blurred the barriers between supply of resources and production of goods and services: "Due to multiple functional interfaces and relation-specific investments, organizational boundaries between supplier and buyer begin to blur. The partners' destinies become tightly intertwined."[21] But what has blurred the conventional corporate boundaries the most is the Internet. "The Net makes it easy for manufacturing types to communicate with marketers. Most of all, the Net makes it easy for a company to conduct an ongoing, one-to-one dialogue with each of its customers, to learn about and respond to their exact preferences."[22]

Third, with economic activity originating at the customer rather than at the production side, the roles of producers, distributors, and

retailers are changing and in some cases retailers are no longer tautological and distributors are eliminated, shortening the supply chain
between producers and consumers (see Exhibit 6.3). In some industries, like the traveling and brokerage industries, retailers and middle
men are eliminated by online and Internet systems. In other industries, like the garment industry, distributors' roles as middle men and
managers of the product-supply chain are strengthened. They work
closely with both retailers and suppliers to better manage the entire
supply line, shortening delivery time and cutting inventory at the
same time. Retailers are "now managing suppliers through us and
are even reaching down to their suppliers' suppliers. Eventually that
translates into much better management of inventories and lower
markdowns in the stores."[23] In a third group of industries that produce complex products that require continuous innovation, low-cost
manufacturing, and quick and prompt delivery, such as PCs and cellular phones, an array of different models are emerging. Dell Computer, for instance, has pioneered a model that has successfully applied
the just-in-time inventory system from the automobile industry to
the computer industry, eliminating distributors and retailers at the
same time. Specifically, the model virtually integrates the company
with its customers and supplies, "stitching" all of them together as if
they all were a single corporation.[24] In this way, the Dell model lets
customers communicate directly online with the company, and the
company to communicate directly online with suppliers to order parts
as and when needed. This means that Dell Computer is responsive to
changing consumer demands without having to be concerned with
inventories and product obsoleteness that are major constraints for
the high-technology industry. Other computer makers, such as IBM,
Compaq Computer, and Hewlett Packard, have followed a different
model that does not necessarily eliminate retailers and even strength-
ens the role of distributors. Specifically, these companies route customers' orders to distributors who assemble the product on behalf of
their customers. Major American computer distributors Ingram Mico,
Vanstar Corporation, and Tech Data Corporation, for instance, assemble PCs and install for major computer makers and software companies. On their part, computer makers design the major parts, market

and guarantee the final product, and are engaged in R&D. Some distributors, like European Micro Holdings, play a different role than those of Ingram Micro and Vanstar Corporation. They scan the globe for the best PC products. "Unlike such big-name players as Ingram Micro Inc. and Tech Data Corp., which sell thousands of products from multiple makers, European Micro offers a short list of items—but at the lowest price available."[25] In a fourth group of industries that produce electric generators and transmitters, corporations have been transformed into systems designers. Asea Brown Boveri (ABB), for instance, has been gradually transformed from multinational manufacturers to a system integrator and network builder. In this sense, the division of entrepreneurship among the network members and the role each plays in the product chain are not fixed, and do not follow a specific model but rather several models.

In short, in network capitalism, the chain of economic activity begins from the bottom, moves from customers to producers, and becomes shorter and tighter. In some cases the role of retailers and distributors is weakened or eliminated, while in other cases it is strengthened or even redefined. Retailers no longer just retail, distributors no longer just distribute, and producers no longer just produce. They all share a collective entrepreneurship that begins with the identification of consumer demands and ends with the delivery of the appropriate product to accommodate that demand. In this sense, economists and business strategists are called upon to come up with new models of business strategy that shift focus from the narrow concept of the division of labor in the production of goods and services to a broad concept of the division of entrepreneurship in the product-supply chain.

To put it differently, the key to successful business strategy for entrepreneurial networks is the efficient and effective allocation of roles among network members in performing all the necessary product-supply operations, not just production. The efficient and effective allocation of roles in turn is a matter of both logistics and of institutions conducive to the community of common fate. But, as discussed in Chapter 3, logistics, hardware, and software technologies that accommodate the efficient and effective communication of a network are transferable across networks. Hardware technologies can be purchased in the market, while software technologies can be taught inside or outside the network. What cannot be purchased or learned are the institutions that create a community of common fate.

NOTES

1. Quoted in Magretta, 1998a, p. 1.
2. Nemeth, 1997, p. 59.
3. Besser, 1995, p. 52.
4. Senge, P. 1994, p. 507.
5. Rarick and Vitton, 1995.
6. Grant, 1998, p. 81.
7. Magretta, 1998b, p. 122.
8. For details, see Arayama and Mourdoukoutas, 1999a, Chapter 8.
9. Besser, 1995.
10. Dyer, Dong, and Chu, 1998, p. 67.
11. Ibid.
12. Dyer and Ouchi, 1993.
13. Lawrence G. Hrebiniak, *The We-Force in Management: How to Build and Sustain Cooperation*, New York: Lexington Books, 1994, p. 100.
14. Roger Schreffler, "Mazda's Synergy Strategy," *Japan Quarterly* 15 (April–June, 1997): 14–19.
15. Kim, C. and R. Mauborgne, "Fair Process: Managing in the Knowledge Economy," *Harvard Business Review* 75 (4) July–August 1997: 65–75.
16. Kathryn D. Martell and Stephen J. Caroll, Jr., "The Role in Supporting Innovation Strategies: Recommendations on How Managers Should Be Treated from an HRM Perspective," *R&D Management* 25 (1995): 18–22.
17. Susan Jackson, "Back to School with a Difference," *Business Week*, 14 September 1998, p. 22.
18. Morita, 1987, p. 79.
19. Magretta, 1998b, p. 2.
20. Ibid., p. 5.
21. Dyer, Dong, and Chu, 1998, p. 71.
22. Schonfield, 1998, p. 116.
23. Magretta, 1998b, p. 2.
24. Magretta, 1998a.
25. Parets, 1998, p. A4.

The Limits of
Collective Entrepreneurship

Nations' real wealth doesn't reside in forests of rubber trees or acres of diamond mines, but in the techniques and technologies for exploiting them.

—Thomas A. Stewart

Collective undertakings of any kind, not merely governmental, become difficult or impossible not only because A may betray B but because even if A wants to trust B he knows that B is unlikely to trust him.

—Kenneth Arrow

Every biological and social organization has its limits and boundaries. Collective entrepreneurship is not an exception to this rule. One of its limitations is the scarcity of the human talent, the limited supply of talented individuals compared to the demand for them. This is particularly the case in high-technology industries where entrepreneurial networks must often integrate complex information (human-talent constraint). Another limitation of collective entrepreneurship is the increasing difficulty of protecting business discoveries from imitation or outright copying, and, therefore, the difficulty in sustaining market rents. This, again, is especially the case for high-technology industries where the discovery and exploitation of new businesses is based on inventions and innovations that are very costly to develop and yet very easy to imitate or even outright replicate (intellectual-property-right constraint). A third limitation of collective entrepreneurship is the eventual diminishing returns associated with an increase in their size (scale constraint). A fourth limitation is the conflict potential associated with the division of entrepreneurship among members and with the assignment of risks and rewards among those members who contributed human capital and those members who contributed physical capital (social constraint).

Addressing the limitations of collective entrepreneurship in more detail, this chapter is in four sections. The first section is a discussion of the human-talent constraint, the second section is a discussion of the intellectual-property-right constraint, the third section discusses the scale constraint, and the fourth section is a discussion of the social constraint.

THE HUMAN-TALENT CONSTRAINT

"We want you at Sun." With signs like this printed on giveaway coffee mugs and T-shirts, high-technology companies like Sun Microsystems have been launching an aggressive campaign to entice engineers to their ranks. Some companies are even more generous than Sun Microsystems, offering much more than mugs for the recruitment and retention of qualified employees: hefty sign-up cash bonuses, country club memberships, brand new cars, relocation allowances, and a generous stock ownership option plan.

Company generosity in recruiting and retaining a qualified labor force reflects the recognition that human talent is the ultimate source of competitive advantage. Indeed, in contrast to physical capital and technology transferable across corporate borders, human talent, the knowledge embedded in people's minds, is not transferable across companies. As Brach puts it, "Increasingly, the wealth of companies is their intellectual capital, and much of that—from a perfume secret ingredient to a big customer's favorite dessert—resides between the ears of a company's knowledge workers."[1] This is particularly the case for entrepreneurial networks that are formed for the purpose of the discovery and exploitation of new business opportunities. After all, entrepreneurial networks are associations of individuals who share some special talents and knowledge.

Yet in every national economy and in the global economy as a whole there is a certain pool of human talents that is drying up, especially in the economies where unemployment is historically low, like the United States. This means that further growth of industries which rely heavily on human talent like the high-technology industries will be constrained by the shortage of such talent. In fact, signs of such a constraint are already eminent. According to a 1998 Coopers & Lybrand survey, 70 percent of high-technology CEOs identified a shortage of highly skilled workers as the major constraint for their growth.[2] According to a 1998 study, more than 346 thousand information-technology jobs remained unfilled due to the shortage of a qualified labor force.[3]

This shortage of human talent in the high-technology industries is further consistent with the 1996–2006 government survey of fastest growing occupations. Employment of database administrators, for instance, is expected to grow by 118 percent over this period; employment of computer engineers by 109 percent; and systems analysts by 109 percent (see Exhibit 7.1).

The shortage in specialized, talented individuals is not confined to the computer and information industries. It extends to MBA holders, especially to those who combine an undergraduate technical degree with an MBA and therefore can better understand and integrate market and technical information. "Companies are very happy with the skills today's MBAs possess. They have a rare mix of financial, technical and communications skills that companies have trouble finding in engineers or other degree holders."[4] A mix of financial and technical information, in turn, is important for the discovery and exploitation of new business opportunities (see Chapter 4).

The shortage of MBAs is not confined to the United States. It extends to other countries around the world, especially to former socialist countries where (market) business education was considered as "reactionary" and banned from mainstream educational institu-

Exhibit 7.1
Fastest-Growing Occupations, 1996–2006

Occupation	Employment Change (%)
Database Administrators,	
Computer Support Specialists,	
and All Other Computer Scientists	118
Computer Engineers	109
Systems Analysts	103
Desktop Publishing Specialists	22
Data Processing Equipment Repairers	52
Engineering, Science, and	
Computer Systems Managers	45

Source: U.S. Department of Labor, *1998–99 Occupational Outlook Handbook, 1996–2006* (Washington, D.C.: U.S. Department of Labor).

tions. This is especially the case in China, which began its transition to a market economy system in 1978, less than a decade after the end of the Cultural Revolution. Specifically, the percentage of economic, finance, and management graduates of all university graduates declined from an average of 10.3 in the period 1928 to 1947 to 2.1 in the period 1966 to 1976, and remained at 3.6 in the period 1977 to 1985.[5] The shortage of professional managers is worse in foreign joint ventures which, in spite of the long efforts, have yet to recruit qualified local managers. That is the finding of an AT Kearney survey, *In Structuring for Success in China*, reported in *ASIAWEEK*, an ironic finding given China's immense population size.[6]

In view of the difficulties that companies have in recruiting qualified employees, it comes as no surprise that a 1997 survey in *Fortune* identified the ability to "recruit, retain, and motivate talented people" as the single most important factor for a corporation to make it to the list of the world's most admired corporations.[7] But how can companies recruit and retain qualified employees?

Certainly, one way is to pay competitive pecuniary and nonpecuniary benefits as discussed earlier. Another way, perhaps even more important, is to create an environment conducive to individual creativity and self-fulfillment, an environment of fair and equitable working conditions. The importance of a fair and equitable working environment for the recruitment and retention of human talent is further confirmed by the 1998 *Fortune* survey of the most admired corporations, discussed in Chapter 6. Specifically, the survey found that a number of what seem trivial policies that eliminate distinctions, such as the elimination of corner offices and separate parking lots, made the difference between the companies that managed to recruit and retain talented people and be included in the list of most admired companies and those who were not. In addition to fair and equitable conditions, Brach proposes a three-stage comprehensive retention plan that lasts several years. First, assign "mentors" to new recruits, senior employees that will assist them to adopt and adapt to their new working environment. Second, once the new recruits adopt and adapt to the new conditions, assign them to challenging projects. Third, after they successfully complete such projects, reward them with stock options.[8]

In short, the ability of entrepreneurial networks to renew and expand their members is constrained by the scarcity of human talents, especially in the high-technology industries that rely heavily on perpetual inventions and innovations for the development of new products and business. The ability of entrepreneurial networks to expand themselves and to retain market rents is further constrained by the difficulty in protecting their intellectual assets.

THE INTELLECTUAL-PROPERTY-RIGHTS CONSTRAINT

For centuries, intellectual-property-right protection has been an important condition for the discovery and exploitation of new business. It secured market rents and provided the incentive for people to pursue them: "In 1838, Abraham Lincoln was asked to identify the three greatest inventions of all time. The one he listed first was not a machine. It had no gears and wires. Rather, he listed patents, the idea of patents, the idea itself, as the first of a handful of mankind's greatest discoveries."[9] According to Lincoln, the patent "added fuel of incentive to the fire of invention." The patent "remains the most elegant definition of the marriage of the mind and marketplace." And the very fact that the Industrial Revolution spread in eighteenth-century Great Britain that had strong patent laws rather than in thirteenth-century China that had no such laws, attests to Lincoln's contentions.

If intellectual-property protection was so important in the past, it is even more important today for entrepreneurial relations that often share intellectual property assets. Nevertheless, protecting property rights is a rather tricky issue for two reasons. First, it is difficult for a country or the world community to come up with legislation that strikes a balance between granting exclusive rights to inventors and innovators and the limiting of monopoly rights that constrain the diffusion of new discoveries to society at large through competition. As Ouchi and Bolton observe, "Any such system represents an adaptation of social, legal, and other forces which yields balance between incentives favoring appropriability granted to inventors and countervailing forces limiting such monopoly grants."[10]

Second, intellectual-property-right laws are difficult to enforce, even in more developed countries such as Japan. As a result, copyright infringement or outright theft is a particularly serious problem for high-technology industries. The situation is even worse in less-developed countries and the former socialist countries in particular, where property rights were not well-defined and where people have been accustomed to consider intellectual property as public goods for free. According to International Intellectual Property Alliance estimates, in 1994 alone, American corporations lost $1.265 billion in copyright revenues in Japan; $866 million in China; $805 million in Russia, and $438 million in Brazil.[11] In 1996, intellectual property theft rose by 323 percent to an estimated $24 billion.[12] In 1997, software piracy alone was estimated at $11.4 billion, with piracy rates in countries like Vietnam, China, Indonesia, Russia, and Turkey reaching 100 percent of the market.[13]

The large size of intellectual-property-right theft outside the United States is not just a matter of law or law enforcement, however. It is a matter of economics, because copying today's high-technology products is far easier and less costly than copying traditional manufacturing products. To understand the difficulties in protecting property rights in today's knowledge and intelligence-intensive industries from those of the traditional labor, capital, or technology-intensive industries, we must recall the new principle of the division of entrepreneurship among the members of collective entrepreneurships in the product-supply chain introduced in Chapter 6.

According to this principle, the success or failure of entrepreneurial business strategies depends on how successfully entrepreneurial networks assign their members to the different operations to be performed in the product-supply-chain operations, namely, R&D, manufacturing, distribution, marketing, and retailing. Modifying this model slightly, we can now assume that the product-supply chain consists of three operations only—invention, innovation, and mass production—with the relative importance of each stage varying by the nature of the product. In traditional capital and technology-intensive industries, the manufacturing component is at par or in some cases even more important than the other two components. Mass manufacturing automobiles, for instance, is, perhaps, as important as developing the prototypes, and mass manufacturing sweaters is more important than designing them (see Exhibit 7.2). This means that the cost of imitating or copying a traditional product is relatively high, as the imitator or copier does have to possess both the engineering skills and the physical-capital equipment. By contrast, in modern information and intelligence-intensive industries, the mass manufacturing component is negligible compared to the other two components

Exhibit 7.2
The Relative Importance of Invention, Innovation, and
Mass Production in Traditional versus Modern Industries

Production Stage	Traditional	Modern Industries
Invention	X	XX
Innovation	X	XX
Mass Production	XX	X

Key: X = important; XX = very important.

(Exhibit 7.2). The mass manufacturing of Windows 1998, for instance, is negligible compared to the other two components—inventions and innovation. This means that the cost of imitating or copying a modern product is relatively low, as the imitator or copier does not have to possess either the engineering skills or the physical capital.

In short, as mass manufacturing assumes less importance in modern industries, the cost of imitation or outright copy of new products is lower than that of traditional industries. This means that entrepreneurial networks would find it increasingly difficult to protect their discoveries and sustain market rents, a condition for their very existence.

THE SCALE CONSTRAINT

As discussed in previous chapters, entrepreneurial networks are conducive both to economies of scale and economies of scope and let their members combine both mass production and customization at the same time (mass customization). This means that the performance of entrepreneurial networks, both in terms of cost and customization, will improve as they grow in size (see Exhibit 7.3). Yet there are good reasons to believe that this cannot go on forever. As was the case with their predecessor, the hierarchical corporation, entrepreneurial networks eventually will run to diminishing returns to scale. This means that their performance will deteriorate as they grow in size. This is especially the case for external entrepreneurial networks that expand across the boundaries of conventional corporations through corporate alliances, for three reasons (see Exhibit 7.3). First, as entrepreneurial networks expand in size, it becomes more difficult for members to communicate with each other and to develop contextual knowledge that allows them to integrate market and technical information for the development of new products.[14] Second, it becomes increasingly more difficult for the network management team to coordinate and monitor the performance of the entire network. In this way, "the quality of ex ante search and ex post monitoring will decline as the firm increases the number of alliances it is involved in."[15] Third, as entrepreneurial networks expand in size, it becomes more difficult for a network to develop a sound vision that holds it together, especially global networks that spread across national and cultural boundaries.

Arguments for the presence of both economies and diseconomies of scale in collective entrepreneursips are supported by studies of strategic alliances in biotechnology industries. Investigating the relationship between the rate of new product development and the number of alliances formed by 132 U.S. biotechnology firms, Deeds and Hill, for instance, found evidence of economies of scale followed by diseconomies of scale. Specifically, the authors found that as the number of alliances increases, the performance (number of new products) of the network initially improves. But as the number of alliances increases further, performance of the network deteriorates.[16]

In short, entrepreneurial networks cannot expand their membership forever. They will eventually experience diseconomies of scale that will limit their growth. But what will limit the growth of networks the most is the conflict among the members of the network; that is, the social constraint.

THE SOCIAL CONSTRAINT

As is the case in every community society, entrepreneurial societies are not always in harmony. The interests of one member are not always compatible with the interest of other members, especially in

Exhibit 7.3
Collective Entrepreneurship: Size versus Performance

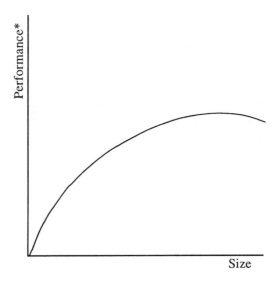

*Performance can be measured in terms of rate of new product discovery or in terms of new business development.

a rapidly changing market environment that changes the role of each member in the product-supply chain. Take the case of entrepreneurial networks in the computer industry as discussed in Chapter 6. Traditionally, computer manufacturers like IBM and Compaq Computer design a new PC, order major components to their suppliers and partners around the world, and assemble the final product where the labor costs are the lowest, normally in Southeast Asia. Then the product is shipped to distributors or directly to retailers around the world. In the meantime, computer manufacturers launch an advertising campaign to entice potential customers to the product.

Today, this model no longer applies in the computer industry, however. As discussed in Chapter 6, computer producers are no longer true producers. Though they still design and advertise new models, they do not order parts, assemble the final product, and ship it to distributors and retailers. Instead, they first receive orders directly from customers, order the parts, and then manufacture the final product, which is directly shipped to the customers (Dell model). Alternatively, computer makers confine themselves to design and marketing, routing customer orders to distributors who also assemble and ship the computers to customers (IBM, Compaq, Hewlett Packard model).

In either case, the shift from the conventional production-supply model to the new product-supply model has turned from a model of harmony to a model of conflict. It has turned former partners into competitors, undermining the spirit of community of common fate, which is the foundation of collective entrepreneurship. Worse, due to the dynamic nature of the computer industry, the new organization models may be proved even more shortlived and less stable than their predecessors. The Dell model, for instance, may compel suppliers to enter into the PC assembly and direct-distribution business to compete head to head with PC producers like Dell. Likewise, distributors in the Compaq and IBM model may develop sufficient knowledge in PC assembly and enter into the PC design and marketing business on their own, again competing head to head with their former partners. In either case, the division of entrepreneurship among existing network members may no longer be incentive compatible. Worse, the potential for former partners turning into formidable competitors may undermine the vision (i.e., the core values and the mission) of networks that create the mutual trust and the incentive compatibility that hold them together.

Another potential source of conflict that may threaten the cohesion of entrepreneurial networks and constrain their growth is the division of risks and rewards among those members who contribute financial capital and those members who contribute human capital. This conflict may become particularly acute in networks whose assets are mostly human; capital is embedded in the members rather than in physical assets detached from them. In such cases, network members, for instance, who contribute mostly human capital are concerned more about personal satisfaction, employment stability, and favorable working conditions, while network members who have contributed mostly financial capital are more concerned for financial returns. How can entrepreneurial networks balance these demands?

Certainly, there are no magical solutions to this problem. Yet entrepreneurial networks can come up with a new governance structure that turns the conventional corporate board from the shareholders' control center to an assignment center that "should decide how to apportion risks and rewards between people who invest money and people who invest themselves."[17] In practice, this means that the assignment center must evaluate and assess the risk tolerance of human-capital owners. Owners of little amounts of human capital, normally low-skilled members, have little tolerance for risk and, therefore, their compensation should include a large fixed component (salary) and a small variable component (bonus, return on equity). By contrast, owners of large amounts of human capital, normally high-skilled members, have high tolerance for risk, and, therefore, their compensation should include a small fixed component and a large variable component (see Exhibit 7.4). Ideally, the board should find a way to let its members decide on their own between risks and rewards. As Stewart puts it, "Like investors who diversify their portfolios, employees should balance risks in their pay packet."[18]

In short, as was the case with conventional corporations, entrepreneurial networks have their own limitations and boundaries that make them timely rather than eternal institutions. First, as the pool of human talent is drying up, it becomes increasingly difficult for entrepreneurial networks to recruit and retain qualified members. Second, as entrepreneurial networks spread over parts of the world where intellectual-property protection is either nonexistent or nonenforceable, it will become increasingly difficult for entrepreneurial networks to sustain market rents. Third, as entrepreneurial networks grow in size, they eventually experience decreasing returns of scale that raise the cost of developing and deploying new business opportunities. Fourth, as market and technical conditions change, the division of entrepreneurship among network members creates winners and losers that threaten cohesion and stability.

Exhibit 7.4
Entrepreneurial Compensation: Human Capital versus Compensation Ratio

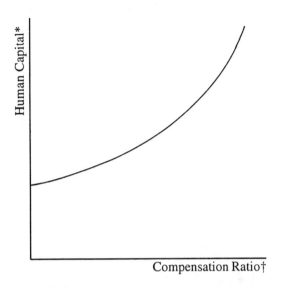

*Human capital can be measured in terms of years of schooling and years of experience.

†Compensation ratio is defined as the ratio of variable pay over fixed pay.

NOTES

1. Branch, 1998, p. 97.
2. Gwynne, 1998.
3. Sears, 1998, p. 130.
4. Reingold, 1998, p. 97.
5. Xu-Yao, Ke-Chun, and Chan-Min, 1989.
6. Healy, 1997, p. 13.
7. Editorial, "America's Most Admired Companies," 2 March 1998, p. 70–75.
8. Branch, 1998, p. 14.
9. Lodewijk, 1996, p. 7.
10. Ouchi and Bolton, 1998, pp. 10–11.
11. Hall and Staimer, 1995, p. A1.
12. Radcliff, 1996, p. 60.

13. "Emerging Market Statistics," *Economist*, 27 June 1998, p. 124.

14. As discussed in Chapter 4, communication is not just a matter of hardware technologies such as information highways, it is also a matter of software technologies, such as job rotation, transfers, and team effort that are not expected to function as efficiently and effectively as an entrepreneurial network grows in size.

15. Deeds and Hill, 1996, p. 41.

16. Ibid., p. 45.

17. Stewart, 1998b, p. 189.

18. Ibid., p. 190.

Chapter 8 ———————————————————————

Summary and Conclusions

It is not the strongest of the species that survives, nor the most intelligent, it is the one that is most adaptable to change.
—Charles Darwin

Embrace change, don't fear it.

—Jack Welch

"There has been a bright and a dark side to globalization for businesses," to paraphrase a quote from Charles Dicken's *A Tale of Two Cities*. The bright side of globalization is about instant communication, economic freedom, open markets, free flow of commodities and resources across national and local markets, and new opportunities in emerging markets. The dark side of globalization is about growing competition, excess capacity, price destruction, and thinner profit margins, not to mention corporate bankruptcies.

In either case, globalization has changed the ways companies are organized and compete with each other. In the late 1970s and the 1980s, a period during which globalization showed more of its bright side, companies began to organize and compete with each other on a number of strategies known as TQC, TQM, and reengineering, strategies that are based on the principle of the division of labor by process, a successor to Adam Smith's principle of the division of labor by task. All three strategies promoted operational effectiveness, to let corporations combine low costs with better quality and better market responsiveness.

In the 1990s, as globalization began to show more of its dark side, operational effectiveness and the strategies and principles that pursue it no longer warrant sustainable competitive advantages, especially to corporations mostly exposed to globalization. In such industries, instead of focusing on strategies of operational effectiveness, corporations must focus on strategies of constructive destruction that abandon conventional business lines that have been invaded by the competition or turned obsolete all together, and transfer resources to new business with little competition. In this sense, a strategy of constructive destruction has two major components. The first component is the management of change (i.e., a strategy that minimizes the friction between winners and losers, spreads the risks and rewards, plans and raises support for change, and balances concentric and centrifugal forces). The second component is the integration of market and technical information for the discovery and exploitation of new business opportunities, a strategy that can be pursued through collective entrepreneurship.

Collective entrepreneurship is a fluid organizational structure that affords the opportunity to the hundreds or even thousands of hidden entrepreneurs scattered among suppliers, distributors, customers, and collaborators to come forward with the information they possess and to join forces for the discovery and the exploitation of new business opportunities. This sort of collective entrepreneurship can take several forms. First, it can be internal collective entrepreneurship (i.e., developed within conventional corporations), by lowering the boundaries among stockholders, managers, and workers. Second, it can be external collective entrepreneurship, by lowering the boundaries that separated producers from their suppliers, distributors, retailers, and customers (vertical external entrepreneurship), and by lowering the boundaries that separated corporations from their competitors (horizontal collective entrepreneurship).

As the internal and external boundaries of conventional corporations are fading away, entrepreneurial networks look more like communities of common fate and less like hierarchical corporations. This means that entrepreneurial networks are held together more by informal rules of conduct and social values rather than by formal rules of conduct and contractual agreements. It also means that a number of business principles that supported and reinforced the business strategies of conventional corporations, such as the division of labor by task (the Taylor system) or by process (the reengineering system), no longer form the foundation of the business strategy of entrepreneurial networks.

Instead, the business strategy of entrepreneurial networks is the division of entrepreneurship, not just in the production operation but among all the operations that make up the product-supply chain; namely, supply of resources, production, marketing, distribution, and retailing. Yet, as was the case with its predecessors, a business strategy of collective entrepreneurship is subject to a number of limitations, including the shortage of human talent, the difficulty in protecting intellectual-property assets, decreasing returns to scale, and the conflict among members over the division of entrepreneurship and the assignment of risks and rewards among members who contribute human capital and members who contribute physical capital.

The first part of this book discussed the characteristics of the dark side of globalization and the limitations of the strategies of operational effectiveness, such as reengineering, TQC, TQM, in competing in the new global market regime. The second part of the book discussed an alternative business strategy, the strategy of the constructive destruction of businesses pursued through collective entrepreneurship and the community of common fate.

Chapter 2 addressed in more detail the other side of globalization, the intensification of competition, excess capacity, and price destruction, and their implications for business strategy. Specifically, in order to survive and prosper in the new global market regime, corporations must reach beyond the managerial revolution brought by reengineering to an entrepreneurial revolution to be brought about by revenue growth through the discovery and exploitation of new business opportunities rather than operational effectiveness and managerial strategies.

Addressing the limitations of reengineering in more detail, Chapter 3 showed that such strategy is no longer a sufficient source of sustainable competitive advantages. Specifically, as was the case with its predecessor, scientific management, reengineering is subject to a number of limitations, such as the increasing difficulties of adoption and adaptation to reengineering policies, imitation, market saturation, and product complexity. Such problems have transformed reengineering into a business strategy of the past, rather than a strategy of the future that takes a completely novel approach to the issue of business strategy and business organization.

Chapter 4 reached beyond reengineering to strategies that expand and enhance revenue growth through the constructive destruction of a corporation's own businesses, particularly to strategic innovations and the integration of market and technical information for the development of new businesses. Specifically, as capitalism is approaching its ultimate frontier, the global economy, and as companies find it increasingly difficult to compete for distant markets as was the case in the earlier globalization, they must compete against themselves. In this way, companies must perpetually abandon competitive products with high degrees of market saturation and replace them with entirely new ones with low market saturation and little competition.

To pursue strategies of constructive destruction, corporations must deal with three problems associated with them: friction between winners and losers, concentric and centrifugal forces, and integration of market and technical information for the discovery and exploitation of new business opportunities. In this way, corporations must transform themselves into collective entrepreneurships and communities of common fate.

Chapter 5 outlines the concept of collective entrepreneurship and compares and contrasts it with individual entrepreneurship. The chapter begins with a discussion of the other function of the firm, entrepreneurship, and proceeds with a discussion of market institutions and entrepreneurship in particular through the various stages of capitalism. Individual capitalism is personal capitalism with the individual owner–manager–entrepreneur at the core of economic activity. Individual industries include independent small-scale firms owned by individual proprietors and partners who perform both a managerial and an entrepreneurial function, and at times work on the side of labor. In this way, individual capitalism is a system with well-defined market institutions. Firms have no internal boundaries to divide owner–entrepreneurs and managers and managers and workers. But firms do have external boundaries that separate them from their competitors, suppliers, distributors, retailers, and customers.

Managerial capitalism is impersonal capitalism with professional managers at the core of economic activity. Individual industries include a small number of large-scale enterprises owned by stockholders and managed by professional managers who seldom perform any direct labor. In this way, corporate capitalism is also a system with well-defined formal institutions. Large corporations have well-defined external and internal boundaries. External boundaries separate each corporation from its suppliers, distributors, retailers, and customers. Internal boundaries separate stockholder–owners from manager–nonowners, and workers.

Network capitalism is a hybrid of personal and impersonal capitalism with collective entrepreneurship at the center of the action. Individual industries consist of entrepreneurial networks owned and managed by their members. In this way, network capitalism is a system of vague and informal institutions (i.e., they do not have well-defined external boundaries). Entrepreneurial networks are alliances of suppliers, producers, distributors, and customers, often alliances among former competitors rather than distinct corporations in the conventional meaning of the term. In this way, entrepreneurial networks are more like communities of common fate and less like conventional corporations.

Chapter 6 connected collective entrepreneurship with the community of common fate and introduced a new principle of business strategy and organization, the division of entrepreneurship in the product-supply chain. Based on this new principle, the sufficient condition for a successful business strategy for entrepreneurial networks is the efficient and effective allocation of roles among network members in performing all the necessary product-supply operations, not just production. The efficient and effective allocation of roles, in turn, is a matter of both logistics and a matter of institutions conducive to the community of common fate. But as discussed in Chapter 3, logistics, hardware, and software technologies that accommodate the efficient and effective communication of a network are transferable across networks. Hardware technologies can be purchased in the market, while software technologies can be taught inside or outside the network. What cannot be purchased or learned is the institutions that create a community of common fate.

Chapter 7 discussed the limitations of constructive destruction management and collective entrepreneurship. Specifically, as was the case with conventional corporations, entrepreneurial networks will eventually run to their own limitations and boundaries, and therefore are timely rather than eternal institutions. One of the limitations of entrepreneurial networks is their inability to recruit and retain new talent indefinitely in view of a limited supply of a talented labor force. The second limitation is their inability to protect their intellectual property. As entrepreneurial networks spread over parts of the world where intellectual-property protection is either nonexistent or nonenforceable, it will become increasingly difficult for entrepreneurial networks to sustain market rents. The third limitation of entrepreneurial networks is decreasing returns to scale. As entrepreneurial networks grow in size, they eventually experience decreasing returns of scale that raise the cost of developing and deploying new business opportunities. The fourth limitation is the social constraint. As market and technical conditions change, the division of entrepreneurship among network members creates winners and losers, which threatens cohesion and stability.

Selected Bibliography

Abo, T. 1995. "Cross-Border Aspects of Foreign Subsidiary Management." *Management International Review* 35: 70–85.

Arayama, Y., and P. Mourdoukoutas, 1999a. *China against Herself: Imitation or Innovation in International Businesses*. Westport, Conn.: Quorum Books.

Arayama, Y., and P. Mourdoukoutas, 1999b. *The Global Corporation: The Decolonization of International Businesses*. Westport, Conn.: Quorum Books.

Arrow, K. 1974. *The Limits of Organization*. New York: W. W. Norton.

Asbrand, D. 1997. "Squeeze Out Excess Costs with Supply-Chain Management Solutions." *Datamation*, 17 March, 62–65.

Baran, P., and P. Sweezy. 1996. *Monopoly Capital*. New York: Modern Reader Paperbacks.

Barreto, H. 1989. *The Entrepreneur in Microeconomic Theory: Disappearance and Explanation*. New York: Routledge.

Baumol, W. 1993. "Formal Entrepreneurship Theory in Economics: Existence and Bounds." *Journal of Business Venturing* 8: 197–210.

Benerza, K. 1997. "7-Up Beats Marketing Drums, but Pepsi Alliance Is in the Offing." *Brandweek Magazine*, 22 September.

Bergson, H. 1911. *Creative Evolution*. New York: Henry Holt and Company.

Berle, A. A., Jr. 1954. *The 20ᵗʰ Century Capitalist Revolution*. New York: Harcourt, Brace and Company.

Berle, A. A., Jr., and G. Means. 1968. *The Modern Corporation and Private Property*. New York: Harcourt, Brace & World.

Besser, T. 1995. "Rewards and Organizational Achievement: A Case Study of Toyota Motor Manufacturing in Kentucky." *Journal of Management Studies* 32: 52–63.

Blackford, M. 1988. *The Rise of Modern Business in Great Britain, the United States, and Japan.* Chapel Hill: University of North Carolina Press.

Blackford, M., and A. Kerr. 1986. *Business Enterprise in American History.* Boston: Houghton Mifflin.

Bok, D. 1993. *The Cost of Talent.* New York: The Free Press.

Bowles, J., and J. Hammond. 1991. *Beyond Quality.* New York: G. P. Putnam's Sons.

Branch, S. 1998. "You Hired 'Em. But Can You Keep 'Em?" *Fortune,* 9 November, 97–100.

Brandt, S. 1986. *Entrepreneuring in Established Companies: Managing Toward the Year 2000.* Homewood, Ill.: Dow Jones–Irwin.

Bridges, W. 1994. "The End of the Job." *Fortune,* 19 September, 62–74.

Brown, S., and K. Eisenhardt. 1997. "The Art of Continuous Change: Linking Complexity Theory and Time-Paced Evolution in Relentlessly Shifting Organizations." *Administrative Science Quarterly* 42: 10–12.

Bulkeley, W. 1996. "Working Together: When Things Go Wrong." *The Wall Street Journal,* 18 November, R6, R25–26.

Capaldo, G. 1997. "Entrepreneurship in Southern Italy: Empirical Evidence of Business Creation by Young Founders." *Journal of Small Business Management* 35: 86–92.

Carlton, J. 1998. "Low and Falling: PC Prices Just Smashed Through the $1000 Barrier. And They Are Not Stopping." *The Wall Street Journal,* 15 June, A3.

Cartwright, D. 1970. "Achieving Change in People." In *Organization Theories,* edited by W. Sexton. Columbus, Ohio: Charles E. Merrill.

Casson, M. 1996. "The Nature of the Firm Reconsidered: Information Synthesis and Entrepreneurial Organization." *Management International Review* 1: 55–94.

Casson, M., ed. 1982. *The Entrepreneur in Economic Theory.* Totowa, N.J.: Barnes and Noble.

Chandler, A. 1990. "The Enduring Logic of Industrial Success." *Harvard Business Review* 90 (2): 130–140.

Clark, D. 1998. "Upgrade Fatigue Threatens PC Profits." *The Wall Street Journal,* 14 May, B1.

Cochran, T. 1977. *200 Years of American Experience.* New York: Basic Books.

Crump, J. 1997. "Strategic Alliances Fit the Pattern of Industry Innovation." *Oil & Gas Journal* 95: 59–62.

Dauphinais, W., and C. Price, eds. 1998. *Straight from the CEO: The World's Top Business Leaders Reveal Ideas That Every Manager Can Use.* New York: Simon & Schuster.

D'Aveni, R. 1994. *Hyper-Competition: Managing the Dynamics of Strategic Maneuvering.* New York: The Free Press.

Davidow, W., and S. M. Malone. 1993. *The Virtual Corporation.* New York: Harper Business.

Day, R. 1908. *The Raid on Prosperity.* New York: D. Appleton and Company.

Deeds, D. L., and C.W.L. Hill. 1996. "Strategic Alliances and the Rate of Product Development: An Empirical Study of Entrepreneurial Biotechnology Firms." *Journal of Business Venturing* 11: 41–55.

DeFillippi, M., and M. Arthur. 1998. "Paradox in Project-Based Enterprise: The Case for Entrepreneurial Networks." *California Management Review* 40: 125–139.

DeGeus, A. 1997. *The Living Company.* Boston: Harvard Business School Press.

Dent, H. 1998. *The Roaring 2000s: How to Achieve Personal and Financial Success in the Greatest Boom in History.* New York: Simon & Schuster.

Dobb, M. 1958. *Capitalism Yesterday & Today.* London: Lawrence & Wishart.

Downes, L., C. Mui, and N. Negroponte. 1998. *Unleashing the Killer Apps.* Boston: Harvard Business School Press.

Doz, L. Y. 1996. "The Evolution of Cooperation in Strategic Alliances: Initial Conditions or Learning Process?" *Strategic Management Journal* 17: 55–74.

Doz, L. Y., and G. Hammel. 1998. *Alliance Advantage: The Art of Creating Value Through Partnering.* Boston: Harvard Business School Press.

Drake, K. 1998. "Firms, Knowledge and Competitiveness." *OECD Observer* (April–May): 24–29.

Dyer, J. H. 1996. "Specialized Supplier Networks as a Source of Competitive Advantage: Evidence from the Auto Industry." *Strategic Management Journal* 17: 271–292.

Dyer, J. H. 1997. "Effective Interfirm Collaboration: How Firms Minimize Transaction Costs and Maximize Transaction Value." *Strategic Management Journal* 18: 535–557.

Dyer, J. H., and W. Ouchi. 1993. "Japanese-Style Partnerships: Giving Companies a Competitive Edge." *Sloan Management Review* Fall: 31–41.

Dyer, J. H., C. Dong, and W. Chu. 1998. "Strategic Supplier Segmentation: The Next 'Best Practice' in Supply Chain Management." *California Management Review* 40 (2): 57–77.

"The Economy Is Changing. Jobs Are Changing. The Workforce Is Changing. Is America Ready?" 1994. *Business Week*, 17 October, pp. 75–105.

"The End of Privatization?" 1998. *The Economist*, 13 June, 19–26.

Fisher, L. 1998. "Post-Merger Integration: How Novartis Became No. 1." *Strategy & Business* 11: 70–78.

Forrest, J. 1996. "Japanese/US Technological Alliances in the Biotechnology Industry." *R&D Management* 24: 24–36.

Galbraith, J. K. 1978. *The New Industrial State*. Boston: Houghton Mifflin.

Galbraith, J. K. 1984. *The Affluent Society*. Boston: Houghton Mifflin.

Ghoshal, S., and A. C. Barlett. 1995. "Changing the Role of Management: Beyond Structure and Processes." *Harvard Business Review* 73 (1): 86–97.

Gould, J. D. 1972. *Economic Growth in History*. London: Macmillan.

Grant, L. 1998. "Happy Workers, High Returns." *Fortune*, 12 July, 81–95.

Grant, R. 1996. "Prospering in Dynamically Competitive Environments: Organizational Capability as Knowledge Integration." *Organization Science* 7 (4): 375–387.

Greenspan, A. 1998. "Market Capitalism: The Role of Free Markets." *Vital Speeches* 64 (14): 7–11.

Gwynne, P. 1998. "Desperately Seeking Scientists at US Technology Firms." *Research and Technology Management* 41: 18–24.

Hall, C., and M. Staimer. 1995. "USA Snapshots: Japan Tops China in Piracy." *USA Today*, 27 February, 1.

Hammer, M., and J. Champy. 1993. *Re-engineering the Corporation*. New York: Harper Business.

Hammonds, K., and K. Kelly, "The New World of Work: Beyond the Buzz Words Is a Radical Redefinition of Labor," Business Week, 17 October 1994, pp. 78–87.

Hansell, S. 1998. "Is This the Factory of the Future?" *The New York Times*, 26 July, 3.1.

Hara, G., and T. Kanai. 1994. "Entrepreneurial Networks across Oceans to Promote International Strategic Alliances for Small Businesses." *Journal of Business Venturing* 9: 42–55.

Harrison, B. 1994. *Lean and Mean: The Changing Landscape of Corporate Power*. New York: Basic Books.

Healy, T. 1997. "Mainland Lessons." *ASIAWEEK*, 14 February, 12–17.

Hébert, R., and A. Link. 1988. *The Entrepreneur: Mainstream Views & Radical Critiques*, 2d edition. Westport, Conn.: Praeger.

Hébert, R., and R. B. Ekelund, Jr. 1980. *A History of Economic Theory*. New York: McGraw-Hill.

Heilbroner, R., and A. Singer. 1984. *The Economic Transformation of America: 1600 to the Present*. 2d ed. New York: Harcourt Brace Jovanovich.

Hemphill, T. 1996. "Enterprise Strategy and Corporate Environmental Alliances." *Business Forum* 21: 16–22.

Hickman, G., and M. Silva. 1987. *The Future 500: Creating Tomorrow's Organizations Today*. New York: NAL Books (New American Library).

Hill, S., J. McGrath, and S. Dayal. 1998. "How to Brand Sand." *Strategy & Business* 11: 22–26.

Hisrich, R. 1986. *Entrepreneurship, Intrapreneurship, and Venture Capital*. Lexington, Mass.: Lexington Books.

Hounshell, D. 1984. *From the American System to the Mass Production: The Development of Manufacturing Technology in the United States*. Baltimore: John Hopkins University Press.

Iansiti, M., and J. West, "Technology Integration: Turning Great Research into Great Products," *Harvard Business Review*, May-June 1997.

Inkpen, A. 1996. "Creating Knowledge through Collaboration." *California Management Review* 39: 123–140.

Ip, Greg. 1998. "Deflation Becomes Worry for Some Firms, Holders." *The Wall Street Journal*, 26 August, C1.

Janeway, E. 1989. *The Economics of Chaos*. New York: Truman Talley.

Josephson, M. 1962. *The Robber Barrons*. New York: Harcourt Brace Jovanovich.

Kaplan, A. D. 1964. *Big Enterprise in a Competitive System*. Washington, D.C.: The Brookings Institute.

Kash, D. 1989. *Perpetual Innovation: The New World of Competition*. New York: Basic Books.

Kent, A. C. 1982. *Encyclopedia of Entrepreneurship*. Englewood Cliffs, N.J.: Prentice Hall.

Kent, A. C. 1984. *The Environment for Entrepreneurship*. Lexington, Mass.: Lexington Books.

Kilby, P., ed. 1971. *Entrepreneurship and Economic Development*. New York: The Free Press.

Kirzner, I. 1984. "The Entrepreneurial Process," In *The Environment for Entrepreneurship*, edited by Calvin A. Kent. Lexington, Mass.: Lexington Books.

Kirzner, I. 1997. "Entrepreneurial Discovery and the Competitive Market Process: An Austrian Approach." *Journal of Economic Literature* 35: 60–85.

Kuratko, D., J. Hornsby, and D. Neffziger. 1997. "An Examination of Owners' Goals in Sustaining Entrepreneurship." *Journal of Small Business Management* 35: 24–34.

Kuttner, R. 1998. "The Net: A Market Too Perfect for Profits." *Business Week*, 11 May, 20.

Leng, T., Y. Wong, and S. Wong. 1997. "A Study of Hong Kong Businessmen: Perceptions of the Role of 'Guanxi' in the People's Republic of China." *Journal of Business Ethics* 15 (199): 749–755.

Leondhardt, J., 1998. "At Northwest, an ESOP in Name Only." *Business Week*, 14 September, 28.

Levenstein, M. 1995. "Mass Production Conquers the Pool: Firm Organization and the Nature of Competition in the Nineteenth Century." *Journal of Economic History* 55: 575–609.

Link, A. N., D. J. Teece, and W. Finan, "Estimating the Benefits of Collaboration: The Case of Sematech," *Review of Industrial Organization, 11* (5) October 1996, pp. 737–751.

Lodewijk, D. V. 1996. "The Values of Trust: The Challenges Ahead for Innovation." *Vital Speeches* 62: 7–10.

Luo, Y. 1997. "Guanxi and Performance of Foreign-Invested Enterprises in China: An Empirical Inquiry." *Management International Review* 37 (1): pp. 60–72.

Magretta, J. 1998a. "Fast, Global, and Entrepreneurial: Supply Chain Management Hong Kong Style." *Harvard Business Review* 76 (5): 102–113.

Magretta, J. 1998b. "The Power of Virtual Integration: An Interview with Dell Computer's Michael Dell." *Harvard Business Review* 76 (2): 72–85.

"Manufacturing Survey." 1988. *The Economist*, 20 June, 4–12.

Marchetti, M. 1997. "Oracle's Peace Initiative." *Sales & Marketing* 149 (12): 22–25.

Mariotti, J. 1998. "Ten Steps to Positive Change." *Industry Week* 1: 1.

Markides, C. 1997. "Strategic Innovation." *Sloan School of Management Review*, Spring, 9–23.

Markides, C. 1998. "Strategic Innovations in Established Companies." *Sloan Management Review*, Spring, 31–42.

Mayer, J., and J. Gustafson, eds. 1988. *The US Business Corporation: An Institution in Transition*. New York: Bellinger.

Miles, G. 1997. "Organizing in the Knowledge Age: Anticipating the Cellular Form." *Management Executive* 11 (4): 7–20.

Mindell, A. 1998. "Computer Training Thrives As Workers Learn—to Earn." *Crain Detroit Business* 14 (31): 24.

Monczka, R., and J. Morgan. 1997. "What's Wrong with Supply Chain Management." *Purchasing*, 16 January, 69–74.

Morita, A. 1987. *Made in Japan*. Tokyo: Weatherhill.

Mourdoukoutas, 1993. *Japan's Turn: The Interchange in Economic Leadership*. Lanham, Md.: University Press of America.

Mourdoukoutas, P. 1995. *How to Compete in the Japanese Market*. Boston: Copley Publishing Group.

Mourdoukoutas P., and S. Kimura. 1999. "Management Control Systems in Globalizing Industries." *European Business Review* 99 (5): forthcoming.

Mourdoukoutas, P., and S. Papadimitriou. 1998. "Do Japanese Companies Have a Strategy?" *European Business Review* 98 (4): 227–234.

Munk, N. 1998. "Organization Man." *Fortune*, 16 March, 28–35.

Nemeth, J. C. 1997. "Managing Innovation: When Less Is More." *California Management Review* 40 (1): 59–75.

Nonaka, I. 1988. "Creating Organizational Order Out of Chaos: Self-Renewal in Japanese Firms." *California Management Review* 40 (4): 57–73.

Nooteboom, B., H. Berger, and N. Noorderhaven. 1997. "Effects of Trust and Governance on Relational Risk." *Academy of Management Journal* 40 (2): 308–339.

Obrinsk, M. 1983. *Profit Theory and Capitalism*. Philadelphia: University of Pennsylvania Press.

Omta, S.W.F. 1998. "Preparing for the 21st Century." *Research and Technology Management* 41: 40.

Ouchi, W., and K. M. Bolton. 1998. "The Logic of Research and Development." *California Management Review* 30 (3): 9–34.

Ozaki, R. 1991. *Human Capitalism: The Japanese Enterprise System as World Model*. Tokyo: Kodansha International.

Parets, T. R. 1998. "European Micro Holdings: Computer Supplier Scouts the Globe for Best Buys." *Investor's Daily*, 12 October, 6, A4.

Pascale, R. T., and G. A. Athos. 1981. *The Art of Japanese Management: Applications for American Executives*. New York: Simon & Schuster.

Pasternack, B., and A. Viscio. 1998. *The Centerless Corporation*. New York: Simon & Schuster.

Patton, J. 1997. "Sidestepping Obsoleteness." *Industry Week*, 3 November, 22–25.

Penrose, E. 1959. *The Theory of the Growth of the Firm*. New York: John Wiley & Sons.

Piore, M., and C. Sabel. 1984. *The Second Industrial Divide: Possibilities for Prosperity*. New York: Basic Books.

Pusateri, C. J. 1984. *A History of American Business*. Arlington Heights, Ill.: Harlan Davidson.

Quinn, F. 1997. "What's the Buzz?" *Logistics Management*, February, 43–48.

Radcliff, D. 1996. "Network Security: Mission Impossible?" *Software Magazine 17* (1) January 1997, pp. 60–66.

Rarick, C., and J. Vitton. 1995. "Mission Statements Make Sense." *Journal of Business Strategy* 16 (1): 28–35.

Ramachandran, K., and S. Ramnarayan. 1993. "Entrepreneurship and Networking: Some Indian Evidence." *Journal of Business Venturing* 8: 18–29.

Reingold, J. 1998. "And Now, Extreme Recruiting." *Business Week*, 19 October, 97–100.

Rifkin, G. 1998. "Competing Through Innovation: The Case of Broderbund." *Strategy & Business* 11: 48–56.

Sayles, J. 1970. "The Change Process in Organizations: An Applied Anthropology Analysis." In *Organization Theories*, edited by W. Sexton. Columbus, Ohio: Charles E. Merrill.

Scase, R., and R. Goffee. 1987. *Entrepreneurship in Europe*. London: Croom Helm.

Schneiderman, A. 1998. "Are There Limits to Total Quality Management?" *Strategy & Business* 11: 35–44.

Schonfield, E. 1998. "The Customized, Digitized, Have-It-Your-Way Economy." *Fortune 138* (6) 28 September, pp. 114–124.

Sears, D. 1998. "Staffing the New Economy: Shortage or Myth?" *HRMagazine* 43 (7): 8.

Senge, P. 1994. *The Fifth Discipline Fieldwork*. New York: Doubleday/Currency.

Sexton, W., ed. 1970. *Organization Theories*. Columbus, Ohio: Charles E. Merrill.

Siwolop K. 1998. "Books Did It for Amazon, but What's Next?" *The New York Times*, 23 August, 28, 3.5.

Smilor, R. 1986. "Building Indigenous Companies: The Venturing Approach." In *Entrepreneurship, Intrapreneurship, and Venture Capital*, edited by R. Hisrich. Lexington, Mass.: Lexington Books.

Snyder, C. 1940. *Capitalism the Creator*. New York: Macmillan.

Stacey, R. 1992. *Managing in Chaos*. San Francisco: Jossey-Bass.

Stewart, T. 1998a. "Knowledge, the Appreciating Commodity." *Fortune* 138 (7), 12 October, pp. 199–200.

Stewart, T. 1998b. "Will the Real Capitalist Please Stand Up?" *Fortune*, 11 May, 189–190.

Stross, R. 1997. "Mr. Gates Builds His Brain Trust." *Fortune*, 8 December, 84–93.

Taylor, W. F. 1970. "The Finest Type of Ordinary Management." In *Organization Theories*, edited by W. Sexton. Columbus, Ohio: Charles E. Merrill.

Tropman, J., and G. Morningstar. 1989. *Entrepreneurial Systems for the 1990s: Their Creation, Structure, and Management*. Westport, Conn.: Quorum.

Tsuchiyama, R. 1996. "Networking for the 21st Century." *Asian Business* 32 (5): 38.

Tyson, K. 1996. "Perpetual Strategy: A 21st Century Essential." *Strategy and Leadership* 26: 12–18.

Uchitelle, L. 1998. "Learning from the Big Booms." *The New York Times*, 28 June, 4.1.

Veblen, T. 1923. *Absentee Ownership and Business Enterprises in Recent Times*. New York: Viking.

Vlosky, R., and E. Wilson. 1997. "Parenting and Traditional Relationships in Business Marketing." *Journal of Business Research* 39: 1–4.

Weber, T. 1996. "The Alliance Between IBM and Storage Tek." *The Wall Street Journal*, 14 August, A7.

Weidenbaum, M. 1996. "The Chinese Family Business Enterprise." *California Management Review* 38 (4): 141–151.

Wessel, D., and D. Harwood. 1998. "Selling Entire Stock! Capitalism Is Giddy with Triumph; Is It Possible to Overdo It?" *The Wall Street Journal*, 14 May, A2.

"What Makes a Company Great?" 1998. *Fortune*, 26 October, 218.

Whitfield, P. R. 1975. *Creativity in Industry*. New York: Penguin.

Winslow, R. 1998. "Missing a Beat: How a Breakthrough Quickly Broke Down for Johnson & Johnson." *The Wall Street Journal*, 18 September, A1, A5–6.

Wysocki, B., Jr. 1996. "'Restructuring' Is Out, Replaced by Growth." *The Wall Street Journal*, 9 December, A1.

Wysocki, B., Jr. 1998a. "Internet Is Opening Up a New Era of Pricing." *The Wall Street Journal*, 8 June, A1.

Wysocki, B., Jr. 1998b. "Pulling the Plug: Some Firms, Let Down by Costly Computers, Opt to 'De-Engineer.'" *The Wall Street Journal*, 30 April, A1.

Xu-Yao, Q., Y. Ke-Chun, and X. Chan-Min. 1989. "An Evolutionary Account of Management Development in China." In *The Challenge to Western Management: International Alternatives*, edited by Julia Davies, Mark Easterby-Smith, Sarah Mann, and Morgan Tenton. London: Routledge.

Yu, A. 1998. *Creating the Digital Future: The Secrets of Consistent Innovation at Intel*. New York: The Free Press.

Zachary, P. 1998. "Yanks in Vogue: For France's Gemplus, the Secret of Success Is Made in U.S.A." *The Wall Street Journal*, 8 June, A2.

Index

ABOUT THE AUTHOR

Panos Mourdoukoutas is Professor of Economics at Long Island University, where he teaches and conducts research on the Japanese and Asian economies. He travels extensively throughout Asia and Europe and holds an appointment at Nagoya University, Japan. Among his various publications are *The Global Corporation* (Quorum, 1999) and *China Against Herself* (Quorum, 1999, with Yuko Arayama).

ISBN 1-56720-289-6

HARDCOVER BAR CODE